Authority and disorder in Tudor times, 1485–1603

Paul Thomas

CAMBRIDGE
UNIVERSITY PRESS

PUBLISHED BY THE PRESS SYNDICATE OF THE UNIVERSITY OF CAMBRIDGE
The Pitt Building, Trumpington Street, Cambridge, United Kingdom

CAMBRIDGE UNIVERSITY PRESS
The Edinburgh Building, Cambridge CB2 2RU, UK
40 West 20th Street, New York, NY 10011–4211, USA
477 Williamstown Road, Port Melbourne, VIC 3207, Australia
Ruiz de Alarcón 13, 28014 Madrid, Spain
Dock House, The Waterfront, Cape Town 8001, South Africa

http://www.cambridge.org

First published 1999
Reprinted 2002

Printed in the United Kingdom at the University Press, Cambridge

Typefaces Tiepolo and Formata   *System* QuarkXPress®

A catalogue record for this book is available from the British Library

ISBN 0 521 62664 1 paperback

Text design by Newton Harris Design Partnership

ACKNOWLEDGEMENTS
Cover, 7, The Royal Collection © Her Majesty The Queen; 18, 25, 63, 72, 87, 107,
Fotomas Index.

The cover illustration shows a detail from the painting, by an unknown artist,
reproduced in full on page 7.

000 15509

Contents

Contents

The question of authority

When Henry VII won the Battle of Bosworth in 1485, there was no outstanding evidence that this victory was more than the latest turn in fortune in the series of skirmishes and slaughters that had characterised the Wars of the Roses and had, indeed, affected politics for the best part of a century. The crown had repeatedly changed hands and it might well do so again. There were plenty of candidates to dispute Henry's tenuous hold upon it.

Where monarchy, the greatest authority in the land, had faltered and might well falter again, the absence of the 'king's peace' had thrown both local authority and private, informal authority into turmoil. However, as the Tudor monarchs sought to establish themselves and regain royal authority, so the scope for government to impose its peace locally in the shires and also to interfere in private family relationships, in sex and in religion might also become extended. These opening chapters will first look at the state of formal authority in England in the late-fifteenth century, and then examine the local and personal inter-relationships that characterised respect, order and hierarchy at ground level.

Ultimately, authority in a formal sense in late-medieval England derived from king, church and nobility. There was, by 1485, a distinct loosening of the bonds of Christendom with the pope's formal authority at its head, as kings and countries sought to redefine their relationship with the papacy and define and extend their regional privileges. There had already been some significant redrawing of the lines between papal and kingly authority in France, Spain and England. Even greater upheavals in the relationships between Rome and the German and English princes were about to happen.

In England, however, it is possible to go back to the end of the fourteenth century and, like William Shakespeare, draw attention to a crucial moment when the natural order of things was thrown out of kilter. Shakespeare's works so often centre on a first act where the natural order is upset, followed by three further acts in which all hell is let loose pending the reconciliations and restoration of order in Act five. It is, therefore, interesting to consider Shakespeare's history plays from *Richard II* on. They tell us a great deal about the 'natural order', about the expectations of Shakespeare's audience regarding lawful authority, and about the Tudors' attempts to establish themselves securely on the throne.

In these plays, Richard II is usurped by Henry IV. The latter establishes himself and agonises as to whether his adult heir, Henry V, will prove a fit king for England. Henry V rejects Falstaff and becomes an English hero. Yet he dies young and without an adult heir. The unfortunate Henry VI is thus doomed to the horrors of regency and civil strife. Edward IV proves every inch a king, yet also dies without an adult male heir. The princes are murdered in the Tower and the 'unnatural' Richard III reigns briefly and calamitously until the natural order can be restored with Henry VII. He duly produces order from chaos and provides England with the adult and glorious Henry VIII.

Shakespeare wisely spared us Edward VI or Mary, or even Gloriana and, like us, he is analysing the fifteenth century with the benefit of hindsight. Yet his play cycle tells us much about the Tudor predicament and about what the public, such as it was, wanted and expected from authority.

The king's peace

Fundamentally, the phrase 'the king's peace' tells us a great deal about the expectations of subjects regarding rulers. Ultimately, royal authority was expected to fulfil two functions. These were to establish the kind of basic law and order at home that would enable English men and women to sleep in their hovels without serious danger of robbery, rapine, fire and sword from villains, vagabonds and other disturbers of the king's peace and to ensure that slumber would remain uninterrupted by visits of Frenchmen, Spaniards, Scots and other ruffianly foreigners. In short, at its most basic, the king's government should offer simple protection from domestic and foreign lawlessness.

Monarchy fails

Given this premise, it can be seen that in the fifteenth century monarchy failed to live up to expectations. It effectively 'lost' the Hundred Years War against France, or at the very least ended it ingloriously. Although England remained safe from outright invasion from foreigners, nevertheless foreign-backed and foreign-based usurpers and challengers did regularly invade these shores well into the reign of Henry VII, while foreign kings, notably Louis XII and Charles VIII of France, were able to meddle in English politics for many years.

Furthermore, the king's peace had broken down at home. Civil strife could range from small-scale skirmish right up to the elimination of thousands of Henry VI's supporters at the Battle of Towton in 1461 – one of the bloodiest days in domestic English military history. Meanwhile, the networks of royal servants and loyalists – the justices of the peace, sheriffs and nobles – and the system of assizes and local courts, which had for centuries enforced the civil and criminal laws, were breaking down under the strain of civil strife. Private armies roamed the land. Juries were systematically intimidated. Overmighty subjects did flourish. Many took a tilt at the crown itself. Authority in England in 1485 was pretty much what the individual made of it.

Monarchy succeeds

Inertia

When Edward IV, or Henry VII, took and maintained the throne, what sustained their authority? Firstly, one should not underestimate the average subject's desire for a quiet life. As we shall see in examining Tudor rebellions, it took real provocation to propel most commoners onto the field of battle, and it was rare to get such individuals to travel more than ten miles to fight for their grievances.

The Divine Right

Secondly, there was a belief in the Divine Right. This was not the sophisticated doctrine it was to become under Henry VIII and the Stuart kings and under the seventeenth-century Bourbon monarchy in France. Rather, both Edward IV and Henry VII could claim that trial by battle had vindicated God's judgement in their favour (a good argument but one that could well rebound when the next successful military challenger arose). Likewise, heredity and divine choice went together, but with so many claimants who possessed royal blood to a greater or lesser degree this, too, was a dangerously adaptable doctrine.

Heredity could count for a lot. Given that all landholding and every relationship between the nobility and the king and between every noble family and its peers depended upon heredity and succession, then the production of adult male heirs to families both noble and royal was an absolutely critical requirement. To fail in this was to invite challenge to authority.

Warriors

Obviously, leadership and indeed military leadership were important. Although it was not strictly necessary for kings to emulate Alexander the Great and ride and speak in the front rank of the army, nevertheless the reputation of Henry V had derived from his warrior status while Richard III had, in fact, fatally led from the front. It is interesting to note Henry VII's good record as a successful military commander, his sensible tendency to delegate the front rank to his seasoned subordinates, and his acute sense that leadership required display and timely expenditure rather than foolish heroics.

The changing role of monarchy

An earlier generation of historians were fascinated by the efforts of Edward IV and Henry VII in seeking to create a 'new monarchy', and went to great lengths to draw out aspects of both innovation and continuity in the methods employed by these kings in administering their estates, managing their money and in directing the legal system. Yet, while there are plentiful arguments to suggest that the administrative practices of both kings owed more to the revival of successful medieval initiatives than to innovative new ones, something indisputably 'new' had happened to the job description of the monarch by the end of Henry VII's reign. After the Battle of Stoke, in 1487, it was no longer necessary for an English king to risk his own person in battle. From then on, to do so was rare indeed and, with Henry VIII and George II, it was often a case of pure martial self-indulgence on the part of the monarch.

The military requirements of upholding the king's peace could be delegated to professional captains. This delegation had always taken place as the equestrian class in Western society had always accepted the notion that the equestrian knight provided horse and fellow soldiers for the king's host as part of the feudal bargain. However, the experience of the Wars of the Roses had suggested an urgent need to reorganise the military relationship between king and nobility. Lancastrian and Yorkist kings learned the hard way that the simple arrangement by which a feudal host of soldiers was raised and led by the nobility in service to the king could end up all too easily in the nobles leading privately raised armies not necessarily loyal to the king. Hence Henry VII paid urgent attention to passing several laws to restrict Livery and Maintenance, that is the practice of nobles clothing and maintaining armed retainers in their own service.[1]

Feudal changes and the cost of war

In fact, some very interesting developments in the art of war and the maintenance of military preparedness occurred between 1485 and 1540 that created all sorts of new problems for the Tudor kings In establishing and maintaining their authority. Improvements in gunpowder and ballistic technology and related developments in siege and fortress warfare revolutionised and vastly increased the costs of such warfare. Similarly, infantry tactics and the need for increasingly well-drilled hosts on the actual field of battle also increased expense, leaving the traditional feudal army as an unwieldy and amateurish relic.

Such changes posed several difficult problems for the Renaissance monarch. He needed to suppress the feudal levies and thus rid himself of the fear of over-mighty subjects and their liveried retainers. Moreover, by appointing such subjects to be captains of increasingly professional and loyal state forces, the monarch was usefully channelling the nobles' energy into harmless activity that was often actually highly supportive of the state. Yet the new arrangement posed difficulties, particularly for English monarchs. It lastingly altered, for example, the military relationship between England and its European neighbours. Up to 1514, perhaps up to the Treaty of London or 'Universal Peace' of 1518, which was negotiated by Wolsey, Henry VII and the young Henry VIII had been able to pose as significant partners, indeed arbiters, in European power politics. Increasingly, however, the Habsburg and Valois dynasties outstripped the English in their ability to put modern armies in the field. When Henry VIII attempted to recapture the glories of his youth in the foreign wars of the 1540s, he brought ignominy and bankruptcy upon his throne and his country. England lacked the population and therefore the sheer tax potential of the great powers. The money question was to prove critical in shaping royal authority and its relationships with all other powers in the land.

Embarrassment and rebellion

The decline of the traditional feudal host led to a simple but stark difficulty for royal authority. From 1536 to 1537, and again in 1549, 1554 and 1569, regional rebellions against the central government proved highly embarrassing and potentially fatal to the monarch, simply because the king or queen could not field an army with which to deter an armed peasantry.

Thus, during the Pilgrimage of Grace in 1536–37, Henry was faced with the acute discomfort of having to humour the complaints of Robert Aske's rebel pilgrims. He and the duke of Norfolk had, humiliatingly, to play for time until troops could be raised. The savage reprisals against the rebels reflected not only that humiliation, but the special need to deter future rebels and to underline the fate that awaited the rebellious.

Similar embarrassment, followed by similar savagery, characterised Elizabeth I's handling of the Revolt of the Northern Earls in 1569. The representatives of royal authority in the North were helpless and forced to sit out the revolt until Elizabeth could raise money from parliament to underwrite the force she eventually put into the field. Her agent, the earl of Sussex, testified to the power of the local earls' mounted tenantry who 'pass in troppes, armed and unarmed, so fast up and down the country that no man dare well stirre anywhere'.[2]

Although it was recognised, even at the time, that Elizabeth had used the opportunity to extort unnecessarily large sums from her parliament, the fact remained that she had lost control over large parts of her realm at a time of extreme internal and external danger for lack of a sufficient standing army. Again, the lowly adherents of a regional rising paid in blood for their temerity in what Fletcher describes as the government's 'orgy of revenge'.[3]

These two examples highlight a fortunate aspect of the relationship between royal authority and the regions. The remote nature of London's authority and the monarch's reliance upon the trustworthiness of middling men such as Robert Aske, and upon great nobles such as Westmorland and Northumberland, could lead to disaster. Nevertheless, distance ensured that a revolt on the periphery, while more likely to happen than closer to home, was more likely to fail. Bluntly, a successful rebellion needed to march on London and coerce or replace the monarch. However, given that rebellions tended to turn upon local loyalties and local grievances, and often had very ill-focused aims, they lacked a strong resolve to go on that long march. When rebels did set out from their locality, the pull of home connections, the fear of the unknown and the inability to take the great leap into full-blooded treason led to a steady desertion from the ranks. This was as true in 1536 for the Lincolnshire pilgrims as it was from 1745 to 1746 for the Highlanders who faltered at Derby, far to the south of their homeland.

However, the precarious military equation upon which central authority was based was revealed to be appallingly precarious in several incidents during the so-called mid-Tudor crisis. It is arguable, for instance, that Edward Seymour lost his position as Lord Protector largely through his foolishness in leaving his rival John Dudley in charge of the only significant army in the kingdom. Seymour had allowed Dudley to lead this force against the western rebels in 1549, leaving himself militarily and thus politically vulnerable. A few years later, Dudley, as the duke of Northumberland, probably lost his gamble in supporting the nine-day reign of Lady Jane Grey due to the paucity of his forces. Much of his mercenary army had been disbanded for lack of funds, while the remaining 2,000 troops deserted as the strength of loyalty to the legitimate queen became clear. Although Queen Mary had absconded to the safety of Suffolk to await events, it is significant that there was no need to make a formal military assault upon London, as it remained sentimentally loyal to the Tudors and hostile to the would-be usurper.

Mary faced the consequences of military embarrassment in 1554, when Sir Thomas Wyatt's ill-organised rebellion came within a whisker of success. This was simply because, starting in Kent and centring on a march upon London, it could pose a lethal threat to the monarchy before there was any chance of putting a credible loyal force into the field to oppose it. Again, only the loyalty of the population of London and a degree of irresolution among the rebels saved the Tudor monarch.

A choice of options

Clearly, then, the relationship of the monarchy to the military was critical to the maintenance of royal authority. For the Tudors it suggested the need either to raise and maintain a standing army, with enormous implications for finance and taxation, or to create a systemic relationship between London and the regions which would at best ensure regional quiescence or, at worst, would so inhibit potential rebels as to buy time for the regime to defend itself. The above examples suggest strongly that the second option was the occasionally risky but essentially practical choice that was made.

Money and absolutism

Certainly, the obvious opportunity for the creation and maintenance of a credible standing force came in the Henrician period, when the wealth accruing from the dissolution of the monasteries might have been diverted to such a purpose. Royal absolutism, by which the king might hope to subordinate all possible competing sources of power to that of the monarchy, would then have become a possibility. Henry VIII fought his wars and the chance was lost, never really to return. European absolutism was, in some cases, able to achieve a virtuous circle, whereby a standing army could enforce the collection of taxes needed in order to maintain such an army, which could enforce royal absolutism. In England, the pretensions of royal absolutism never raised the funds to maintain the army needed to collect the taxes to maintain absolutism. It was an important loss for the Tudors and for their Stuart successors.

Even though the monarch need not necessarily attend the field of battle, certain aspects of medieval kingship remained valid.

The display of the outward trappings and personal characteristics of kingship was important. Just as Edward IV had confirmed monarchical stability through the richness of apparel and display in his court, underpinned by suitably judicious financial management, so, too, did the canny Henry VII, though the latter's canniness may well have lapsed into ill-judged parsimony. It is notable that Henry's son achieved immediate popularity not only for his extravagance, but for his martial prowess and athletic obsessions. Such display was a necessity on the stage of Renaissance monarchy, hence the excess of the Field of the Cloth of Gold in 1520, when Francis I of France and Henry VIII of England vied with each other in demonstrations of luxurious exhibitionism and displays of regal wrestling and jousting. (Such anachronistic chivalry could be dangerous, as the death of one of Francis's successors in a joust was shortly to confirm.)[4]

The Field of the Cloth of Gold, 1520. This meeting between Henry VIII and Francis I of France was an example of the pomp invested in early modern monarchy by two Renaissance monarchs. What does this lavish display tell us about the theory of the Divine Right of Kings?

Status, esteem and regicide

Meanwhile, the brutal disposal of royal rivals did not cease altogether, but its practice suggested a distinct change in the nature of royalty. Thus, Henry VII was willing to tolerate the survival of pretenders such as Perkin Warbeck and Lambert Simnel, and even of legitimate rivals such as the earl of Warwick, for years on end. Likewise, Mary Tudor prolonged the life of Lady Jane Grey, and Elizabeth never really reconciled herself to the death of her cousin, Mary Queen of Scots.

In some ways, all European monarchs had achieved a level of esteem which made the miserable deaths in imprisonment of earlier kings such as Richard II and Henry VI seem anachronistic. Certainly, the confusion of Charles V over how exactly to treat the captured French king, Francis I, after the Battle of Pavia in 1525, suggests that a captured king could only prove an untouchable embarrassment to his royal captor. A similar predicament was thrust upon Elizabeth I by the flight from Scotland in 1568 of Mary Queen of Scots.

Until the papal bull excommunicating Elizabeth in 1570, the notion of regicide was deeply abhorrent. Elizabeth shrank from it, as had Charles V. It was too dangerous and too de-legitimising an idea to encourage. Later episodes, such as the parliamentary forces' awkwardness in possession of King Charles I from 1646–48, and the terrible fate of Damiens, the would-be assassin of Louis XV of France, who was tortured to death for the deterrence and entertainment of the Parisian crowd, re-emphasised the progress that early modern monarchy made in creating an aura of otherness and inviolability around the monarch's person. Conversely, possession of royal blood, particularly under Henry VIII, could be fatal indeed. The de la Pole family was laid waste in the first half of the sixteenth century, with Henry's thoroughness encompassing even the judicial murder of the harmless countess of Salisbury. Likewise, the duke of Buckingham in 1521 and the earl of Surrey in 1547 paid with their lives for the distinction of their bloodline.

Absolutism and central power versus regional resistance

Clearly, throughout Europe, and to a very significant degree in England, monarchy was changing and developing the nature of its authority.

It seems that the early modern state could go one of two ways, possibly even three. Changes in society, religion and the economy affected the pretensions not only of the monarchy but of all other forms of authority within a given state. Thus, inevitably, royal and centralising pretensions provoked provincial and alternative sources of authority to react. Hence, Tudor success involved bloody clashes and political trials of strength with provincial forces, most notably in the example of great earls such as Norfolk, Westmorland and Northumberland. Similarly, in France, the growing power of the monarchy came at the expense of Brittany, Burgundy and the other *pays d'état*. One way forward for the early modern state was towards successful absolutism, ultimately the achievement of the Bourbon kings of France. Yet this achievement required the imposition of a state religion, and the survival of the monarchy through the protracted upheavals of the Wars of Religion and the civil disturbances known as the *Frondes*.

At first, England seemed bound upon this course, as Henry VIII crushed rebels and potential claimants to the throne and as the Tudors generally seemed to generate a successful mystique of royal absolutism that culminated in the reign of Elizabeth as Queen Gloriana. She held sway, significantly, in partnership with the episcopal officers of a state religion. Yet, thanks to the parliamentary struggles of the following century, the English state took a different path from both the French and the Spanish and veered towards constitutionalism. The extreme example of such a path can be seen in the fate of the state, or non-state, of Poland, where successful noble and particularist resistance to monarchy and central authority led to the helplessness of elective monarchy and the partition of the state itself in the eighteenth century. Exceptionally, of course, the religious upheavals of the sixteenth century provided for a third way exemplified by the theocracies and republics in Switzerland, the Netherlands and even, from 1649 to 1660, in England.

Document case study
Kingship and disorder

1.1 The death of Richard III

The citizens of York, Richard III's former stronghold, give their reaction to his death

King Richard, late mercifully reigning upon us . . . with many other lords and nobility of these northern parts, was piteously slain and murdered, to the great heaviness of this city.

Source: R. Davies (ed.), *York records: Extracts from the municipal records of the City of York*, London, 1843, p. 218

1.2 The Wars of the Roses

A contemporary historian, Polydore Vergil, gives an account of the Wars of the Roses

This, finally was the end of foreign war, and likewise the renewing of civil calamity; for when the fear of outward enemy, which as yet kept the kingdom in good exercise, was gone from the nobility, such was the contention among them for glory and sovereignty, that even then the people were apparently divided into two factions . . . their two factions grew shortly so great through the whole realm . . . that many men were utterly destroyed, and the whole realm brought to ruine and decay.

Source: H. Ellis (ed.), *Three books of Polydore Vergil's English history*, Camden society, 1844, pp. 93–94

1.3 The failings of Henry VI

Polydore Vergil on Henry VI

In this same time the realm of England was out of all good governance . . . for the king was simple and led by covetous counsel, and owed more than he was worth . . . all the possessions and lordships that pertained to the Crown the king had given away, some to lords and some to other simple persons so that he had almost nought to live on.

Source: H. Ellis (ed.), *Three books of Polydore Vergil's English history*, 1844, pp. 79–80

1.4 Edward IV takes action

From the Chronicle of Croyland Abbey written by the monk Ingulph, 1475

Others took to pillage and robbery, so that no road in England was safe for merchants or pilgrims. Thus the lord king was compelled to perambulate the country together with his judges, sparing no-one; even his own servants received no less than a hanging if they were detected in theft or murder. Such rigorous justice, universally carried out, put a stop to common acts of robbery for a long time to come.

Source: H. T. Riley, (ed.), *Ingulph's Chronicle of the Abbey of Croyland, 1475*, in Denys Cook, *The sixteenth century, documents and debates*, Basingstoke, 1996, pp. 9–10

1.5 The kingship of Henry VII

Polydore Vergil on Henry VII

His hospitality was splendidly generous . . . But to those of his subjects who did not do him the honour due to him he was hard and harsh. He knew well how to maintain his royal dignity and everything belonging to his kingship, at all times and places. He was most successful in war, although by nature he preferred peace to war. Above all else he cherished justice and consequently he punished with the utmost vigour, robberies, murders and every other kind of crime.

Source: H. Ellis (ed.), *Three books of Polydore Vergil's English history*, 1844, pp. 145–47

Document case-study questions

1 What does the notion in 1.1 that Richard had been 'piteously slain and murdered' suggest about the North's sympathies?

2 How far did 'foreign war' mentioned in 1.2 enable the early Tudors to keep their nobles safely distracted and occupied?

3 To what extent had the kings of England failed to maintain 'the king's peace' during the fifteenth century, and why? Use 1.2, 1.3 and 1.4 to support your conclusion.

4 In 1.5 the author comments that Henry VII was 'successful in war'. Why was this so significant a factor for Henry?

5 Use 1.3, 1.4 and 1.5 to compare and contrast Edward IV's and Henry VII's methods of kingship with those of Henry VI.

Notes and references

1 See R. Lockyer, *Henry VII*, London, 1990, p. 26.

2 A. Fletcher, *Tudor rebellions*, London, 1983, pp. 85–89.

3 Fletcher, *Tudor rebellions*.

4 Henry II of France perished from injuries received in a joust, precipitating the succession of the sickly and shortlived Francis II and the kind of succession and regency problems in France which had previously worried the English monarchy.

2 Law and power

The king wielded both legislative and judicial power: the first through power of proclamation and indirectly through parliament, the second through several courts that had developed to reflect different royal functions, for example those of a landowner, an arbiter of affairs, or an administrator of the country as a whole. The monarch was the ultimate source of appeal for justice, derived authority from his own estates, and also stood at the apex of a system of common law that had gradually become established since Plantagenet times.

The changes that affected the legal system in England and Wales and altered the nature of royal authority in the sixteenth century derived, in part, from simple change in the number and structure of the courts and in their function and popularity. They also came from the nature and effectiveness of the partnership between the monarch in London and his administrative and legal agents in the provinces. In looking at the successful (or otherwise) exercise of royal authority from the bottom up, it is quite possible to argue that the re-establishment of royal authority at local level by Henry VII's sheriffs and justices of the peace was the essential building block upon which the Tudor monarchy was to rest.

The courts

It was vital for the king's legal agents or his courts to be successful and to do this they had to compete with other sources of authority and law. The fundamental problem of law and order during the Wars of the Roses had been the ability and willingness of local magnates to set aside the king's writ, and to intimidate and override his agents in favour of their own 'law' and interests. There were four ways in which a new king could tackle this problem of local loyalty.

Royal progress

One way that was favoured by Edward IV and his brother Richard III was to use the royal progress around the provinces. They accompanied the quarterly circuit courts to administer justice and in order to be seen to administer justice. In Richard's case, he was rather obviously and personally seeking to rebut the sinister rumours of tyranny and infanticide that clung to him. The progresses of the Tudors likewise sought to display their persons, the trappings of royalty, and to reinforce the administration of justice.

Loyal personnel

A second approach, in many ways as obvious as the need for personal display, was the need to make wholesale changes of personnel to accompany a change of regime. There was, of course, a high degree of continuity in those who held office as local justices of the peace. Not all were delinquent, and an example such as Sir Richard Danvers, who held office in Nottinghamshire from 1453 to 1486 without offence to the many different regimes in London, was unlikely to be unique. Furthermore, the nature of local ties, wealth and obligation necessarily restricted the choice of personnel available to the monarch.

Reforming legislation

One way around this problem of personnel was to be found in Henry VII's repeated legislation to change and reinforce the role of the justice of the peace at the expense of the sheriff. This bypassed a number of unsatisfactory personnel and strengthened the flexible and increasingly important institution of local justiceship.

New and prerogative courts

Finally, a king could create new institutions either on an ad hoc or permanent basis which would replace or override other local authorities.

The first two Tudors revived and reinforced the regional extensions of the royal Council in the North and in the Marches, with Henry VIII going further to achieve the Union of England and Wales. His minister, Thomas Cromwell, also revitalised the administration of the *Valor Ecclesiasticus*, the county-by-county survey of church wealth, intimidated local Grand Juries, and introduced tax commissions in order to bully northern and eastern churches and authorities during the Reformation of the 1530s. Furthermore, another specialist committee of the council, that of the Star Chamber, was used by Henry VII, and later by Wolsey, very specifically as an executive or prerogative court. It had powers to summon and constrain local magnates through jurisdiction over local property disputes.[1] This latter court, particularly, illustrates the importance of regular usage or popularity which could cause a court to thrive.

While detested by the magnates who suffered from its attentions, the Star Chamber seems to have been a popular avenue of redress for lowlier plaintiffs seeking judgements against the higher ranks of society. Wolsey, the son of an Ipswich butcher, was happy to oblige them and likewise expanded the prestige and activity of the Court of (Poor Man's) Requests which increased its number of cases and gained popularity as an avenue of redress for commoners.

The centre of the legal system lay, of course, in London and, at least until the fall of Wolsey, the key to power for the king's most ambitious administrator lay in gaining offices and power within the law courts. Morton, Warham, Wolsey and More, however, received their training and their first advancements through an educational and administrative start in the great religious households, and with a substantial grounding in canon law. It is significant that, thereafter, Cromwell, Petre, Paget, Burghley and others were distinctly secular figures, lawyers still, but lawyers chiefly versed in the technicalities of the bureaucracies set up or adapted by Cromwell himself.

Justice within the counties

County and nobility

However, though the law centred upon London, 'local political rivalries generally revolved around control of the lieutenancy and the commission of the peace',[2] that is around the administrators of justice at county level.

Meanwhile, the quarter sessions had become 'a lynch-pin of county government' by 1558. The justices of the peace were themselves substantially affluent figures in the county, with the lord lieutenant, usually a privy councillor or senior grandee, administering through a number of deputies and captains. Given that justices were unpaid for their services, the initiative for service and for competition in local politics came from the need for political advancement, local respect, recognition and promotion for loyal service, and from a desire for the exercise of raw power through office and patronage. With counties administered more or less uniformly under the system of lieutenancies from 1485, it was critical that each monarch should achieve a balance between patronage, power and loyalty. The Yorkists had sought to buy loyalty through grants of land and office, only to see magnates such as Clarence, Buckingham, Northumberland and Stanley change sides. Under Henry VII such grants became rare, the royal demesne was preserved and patronage and promotion had to be earned. The resulting mixture of carrots and sticks inevitably created some bad losers. Thus, the Stanleys changed sides again after Bosworth, while Wyatt's Rebellion under Mary Tudor highlighted the trouble that could be caused by royal thoughtlessness. In 1554, Wyatt himself and Sir Peter Carew in the West Country were prime examples of loyal 'county' figures who had done sterling work for Mary in ensuring the continued allegiance of the provinces in her favour, only to find themselves (in their view) passed over for promotion by the influx of Spaniards on the occasion of Philip II's marriage to the queen.

General surveyors, commissioners and the nobility

In maintaining a stable balance between the necessary delegation of local administration to the local great and good, and the equally necessary maintenance of due authority over the counties and nobility, the crown increasingly used its prerogatives. This was partly to reduce the power of the nobility, punish their transgressions and interfere in local affairs, while equally accruing wealth and physical power at the expense of the local elites, not least by enthusiastically exploiting feudal incidents. As ever, balancing such interference without goading the elites into defiance could be fraught. Henry VIII's immediate elimination of his father's notorious servants, Empson and Dudley, at the beginning of his own reign emphasised his awareness that the old king had allowed such servants and the prerogative courts and commissions that they had exploited to overstep the mark in harassing the nobility.

In doing so, Henry VII had been following in the footsteps of Edward IV, who had been happy to use attainders, outlawries and wardships to add land to the royal estates (and as often over-generously to bestow them upon unreliable supporters). However, Henry VII appointed his administrators as general surveyors to pursue claims actively, interfere in their disputes and to dig up the distant past in order to harass the elites. The use of devices such as bonds, or recognisances, for future good behaviour disciplined the nobility, but it did not endear Henry's regime to them.[3]

As mentioned above, Henry and his successors sought to reduce the retaining of private armies to manageable proportions. Laws on Livery and Maintenance were only partly successful and, besides, the Tudors needed their nobles to raise troops for them. Eventually, the reorganisation of county administrations around the lieutenancies changed the nature of the feudal host and provided forces of varying qualities to meet the threats of foreign invasion that bedevilled the reigns of Henry, Mary and Elizabeth. The county musters raised by the lords lieutenants were slow in gathering but they were preferable to the retained private armies of the Wars of the Roses.

The parishes

Parish and county

For the bulk of Tudor subjects, at least outside London's immediate sprawl, it was the parish that formed the closest and most intimate unit of government and order. In the Middle Ages the parish church and the manorial court had been the twin hubs of the immediate administrative universe. Although the sixteenth century was to see revolutionary changes in religion, the parish church would remain a bedrock institution of the early modern state. However, the relationship between the individual and his or her position within the parish, and the individual's own morality, was to be very much altered over the course of the English Reformation.

It is impossible to remove the spiritual or moral element of parish affairs from discussion of the parish as a political and social source of authority. Recent research embodied in *The experience of authority in early modern England*[4] highlights the role of the parish in such diverse areas as local politics, the reformation of manners, the role of households, women and juvenile delinquents and, of course, in the keeping of the king's peace. Whether pre-Reformation or post-Reformation, Catholic or Church of England, the parish represented in a formal sense a network of families and individual souls and reflected both their formal religious beliefs and their informal fears and prejudices.

Although much of the history of the Reformation reflects the enormous pressure from above to conform to the religious changes of the moment, any realistic view of the acceptance or rejection of religious, social, economic or political change during the turbulent sixteenth century must include comment on reaction at parish level. Not least, it is imperative to remember the very great degree of practical independence from day-to-day interference that the provinces enjoyed from the government in London, and also the very great degree to which parish government led London in its formulation of responses to the various social difficulties experienced as a result of change.

Parish justice and community welfare

The parish was the first line of defence for a community beset by basic problems of unneighbourly behaviour, petty crime, violence, immorality and witchcraft. A great deal of summary justice was meted out within an offender's immediate community, perhaps to a scolding wife, a notorious parish adulterer, or, increasingly, a suspected witch. This could be done by the exemplary violence of stocks or pillory, or the expression of neighbourly disapproval in the form of 'rough music', when offenders were taunted with noisy disapproval or were ostracised. Not least, there is plenty of recent evidence that church courts and parishes increasingly interacted to impose a stricter moral code on the commons as the century progressed.[5]

Until 1536, the role of the parish priest, the local monastery and the existing framework of Catholic theology constituted vital and familiar elements in alliance with parish authority. So did Catholic practice with its array of sacraments, penances and its dependence on the intercessions of the priest or of a particular saint on behalf of the worshipper. In some ways, the priest's role within the parish, and his status, may have increased after the Reformation which had, after all, sought to improve standards of education, ability and accountability in the priesthood, and to eliminate dead wood. However, the turbulence of the reforming process, the uncertainty caused by seemingly endless change and the repeated and pointed attacks upon clerical standards must have also done much to undermine such authority.

Moreover, whatever the priest's civic status, the loss of the comfort of Catholic Intercession, and more materially of almsgiving and monastic hospitality, left the civil powers of the parish to deal squarely with problems of indigence, beggary, vagrancy and old age. These were, in the recessions of the middle and end of the century, of a more acute order than ever before experienced. Put simply, the role of the parish had to expand out of sheer necessity in order to continue to assert moral and orderly standards and to tackle material needs and welfare in an ever harsher world. When central government, from Wolsey's commissioners through to Cromwell's law by which persistent vagrants could be enslaved, and on into the comprehensive Elizabethan Poor Laws, sought to relieve the outstanding welfare problems of the time, they could look to a range of county and parish measures. The fundamental structure of poor relief was based on the parish, which would offer relief only to its own parishioners and to no other. The parish provided the essential control against vagrancy. Its workhouse offered relief, its beadle or constable provided coercion of one kind or another. Yet authorities in towns such as Norwich independently stockpiled food to offset shortages and to pre-empt the danger of food rioting. If indigence and vagrancy provided an affront to the Tudor sense of order, the localities provided frontline remedies. As genuine economic crisis loomed, it was up to the central government, through parliamentary legislation, to offer national and uniform remedies. Naturally, governments took up methods that had already been tried and tested in the parishes and provinces of the land.

Parliament

Status and business

The status of parliament changed dramatically under the Tudors. Where Edward IV's reign had been described as 'one of the least constructive and inspiring phases in the history of the English parliament' and Henry VII's as 'one of the dimmer periods of parliamentary history',[6] the Tudor era ended with the apparent victory of parliamentary pretensions in the 'Monopoly' debates of Elizabeth's last parliaments, to be followed notoriously by the vicious, ultimately fatal struggles between the House of Commons and the first two Stuart kings.

The change in relative status and business of Lords and Commons by the end of the sixteenth century certainly illustrated an important change in the distribution of political power. By 1600, the kind of gentry, knights of the shire, justices of the peace and lawyers who made up the Commons found it a useful instrument for expressing their opinions and their political and economic grievances, as well as a ready vehicle for their political ambitions.

Parliament had been of acute political importance before, notably in Richard II's reign, when its status as a major court was hijacked by Richard and then by his enemies, both using the procedure of parliamentary impeachment to eliminate each other's enemies and to further their respective political goals. Parliament's judicial functions had then languished, passing to the king's conciliar courts, although impeachment was soon to be revived with momentous consequences in the reign of James I.

Functions and frequency

The status of recent kings had been ratified by parliament, a useful ploy by successful usurpers. Winners passed acts of attainder to confirm and justify the transfer of lands from losers. Such transactions necessarily occurred early in a reign. Otherwise Edward IV and Henry VII had little recourse to parliament. Henry held only two parliaments for a total of perhaps 120 days between 1497 and 1509. Such lack of business or frequency militated against members of parliament in either House acquiring the experience or organisation to be effective politically. Partly this was because neither Edward nor Henry needed, nor allowed themselves to need, money from parliament to any significant extent. Troubled at home, both kings were understandably reluctant to court the sort of trouble which might necessitate the grant of funds from parliament. They avoided foreign war, and were anxious to build up the royal demesne and revenue specifically to avoid the kind of money troubles and diminishing patronage base that had so damaged Henry VI. A useful by-product was that such unaccustomed affluence obviated the need to call parliament.

The Reformation Parliament and beyond

From 1529 onwards, Henry VIII co-opted parliament into his assault upon the church. However one views the origins and motives behind the English Reformation, there is no doubt that an essential trigger for the whole process was Henry's desperate need to obtain a divorce in order to marry Anne Boleyn. This need triggered a dispute with the papacy and with the church's representatives in England – Convocation. Whatever the details, the ease with which Henry's harassment of Convocation, in alliance with the anti-clerical members of parliament, led to the levying of a massive fine upon the church, set up a vastly tempting way forward for both king and parliament. In alliance with parliament, in fact operating specifically, legally and constitutionally as 'king in parliament', Henry VIII stood to gain in three ways. First, he got his divorce and married Anne Boleyn. Meanwhile, the long struggle had opened up two other immense gains: in money, treasure and land from looting the estates of the church and monasteries and, by taking on the mantle of papal authority itself, a straightforward accretion of authority as Supreme Head of the Church of England. Setting aside the spiritual implications of the break with Rome, Henry was setting out to break up and then absorb a great rival source of wealth and power in England – that of the late medieval church. The implications of this for kingly and ecclesiastical authority will be examined shortly. In the meantime, the decision to assault the church, and the process of carrying through that assault in association with parliament and in self-interested alliance with the classes represented by parliament, meant that those classes and that institution were also going to make outstanding gains in partnership with the king and at the expense of the church.

The use of statute

The books of G. R. Elton lastingly set out the huge contributions made by Thomas Cromwell to the development of early modern government. His *The Tudor revolution in government* of 1953 drew attention to the vastly increased use and importance of statute law from the Reformation Parliament onwards. One of the most striking aspects of the period was Thomas Cromwell's willingness, acting as Henry VIII's chief minister, to use parliamentary statute to 'nail down' each plank of the Reformation process.

Thus, anti-clerical statutes from 1529 to 1530 marked the start of the assault on the church, and the 1533 Act in Restraint of Appeals and the 1534 Act of Supremacy detailed the shift of papal power from Rome to Henry as Supreme Head of the Church. The Six Articles of 1539 then defined the spiritual content of what, for the time being, the Church of England professed to believe. Yet the process of breaking with Rome took statute and parliament's alliance with Henry into deeper waters, as the need to legitimise and then de-legitimise Anne Boleyn's daughter, Elizabeth, led to Acts of Succession and statutory oaths of loyalty. Furthermore, the need to organise and administer the process of looting and the absorption of church and monastic wealth led to a whole series of further statutes which ratified the authority of the 'new' revenue courts

A woodcut showing children in school. The attack on the church was accompanied by the redistribution of much ecclesiastical wealth into education, which became more secular and humanist. To what extent did the Tudors redirect and 'tame' the ambitions of the sixteenth-century ruling classes?

rationalised by Thomas Cromwell, for example the Court of Augmentations and the Court of First Fruits and Tenths. These were backed by statutes that asserted their authority through parliament to administer the wealth arising from the royal seizure of monastic wealth and annates (the first fruits or first year's income from a benefice) and tithes (tenths) respectively.

One need not necessarily accept the whole of Elton's theory concerning a Tudor Revolution. Indeed, the supremacy of statute in the Reformation era, and beyond, should probably be advanced as the simple extension of the process of ratification we have noted with the coronation of successive kings and their use of attainders back in the fifteenth century. However, by involving parliament in ratifying the break with Rome, the seizure of church and monastic assets, the succession to the throne and the minutiae of government bureaucracy, Henry and Cromwell were consciously or unconsciously bringing the Houses of Commons and Lords into partnership with the crown with lastingly significant consequences.

Firstly, the Reformation Parliament convened for repeated and lengthy sessions for the whole of the period from 1529 to 1536. Frequency and length of sitting and the enormous importance of the subjects on which members drafted, debated and legislated increased their sophistication, experience and organisation. Henry was careful to maintain the sense that members were only able to debate subjects as high flown as religion, the succession and foreign affairs on the specific invitation of the king. Cromwell, himself, was careful to involve himself in the detailed drafting and passage of the legislation. The king was at an apex of power, prestige and vigour, and was not above striding down to Westminster Hall in person, as he did during the debates on the Six Articles when, as an anonymous member of parliament said, he 'confounded us all with his wisdom'. However, he lost Cromwell, and the king aged and declined visibly in the 1540s, while in the chaotic sittings of the 1550s when the succession and, indeed, the very religion of the state were again in dispute, parliament would predictably challenge any restriction on its terms of debate. Moreover, the fortunes of nobles, gentry and bureaucrats who were involved in the plundering of the English Catholic church were transformed by the resulting acquisitions of money, land and power. Whether or not there had been a revolution in government, the alliance against the church had spawned a generation of newly promoted and powerful figures such as Sir Richard Rich, Thomas Wriothesley and Thomas Audley who had all worked for Cromwell in the 1530s and were to be found as senior figures in mid-Tudor governments. There had been a qualitative and quantitative shift in money and power with consequent changes in who wielded authority, and how authority was viewed by those subject to the central government and its local allies.

Document case study

Bonds and recognisances, juries, retainers and the Star Chamber

2.1 A recognisance

A recognisance of 1505 by Henry Lord Clifford. A bond or recognisance was a sum of money pledged by a nobleman to the king as a promise of good behaviour. The terms were used interchangeably.

16 June 1505: [Recognisance] for £2,000 by Henry, Lord Clifford. Condition: Henry to keep the peace for himself and his servants, tenants and 'part takers' especially towards Roger Tempest of Broughton, and endeavour to bring before the King and his Council within 40 days such of his servants as were present at the late pulling down of Roger's place and house at Broughton.

Source: *Calendar of the close rolls*, vol. 2, no 499, quoted in R. Lockyer, *Henry VII*, London, 1990, p. 86

2.2 A bond

A bond of 1505 made by George, Lord Burgavenny, with the king

24 December 1507: Indenture between the King and the same George, Lord Burgavenny: whereas George is indebted to the King in £100,000 or thereabouts for unlawful receivers done, retained and made by him in Kent . . . the King may attach his body and keep him in prison and take all the issues of his lands till the whole sum be paid; the King is graciously contented . . . to accept as parcel of the debt the sum of £5,000 payable over ten years.

Source: *Calendar of the close rolls*, vol. 2, no 499, quoted in R. Lockyer, *Henry VII*, London, 1990, p. 86

2.3 The Star Chamber under Cardinal Wolsey

Wolsey to Henry VIII, 1517–18 (letter)

And for your realm, the Lord be thanked, it was never in such peace or tranquillity; for all this summer I have had neither of riot, felony, nor forcible entry, but that your laws be in every place indifferently ministered, without leaning of any manner. Albeit there hath lately, as I am informed, been a fray between Pygot, your servant and Sir Andrew Windsor's servants, for the seisin [right of ownership] of a ward whereto they both pretend titles; in which fray one man was slain. I trust at the next term to learn them the law of the Star Chamber, that they shall ware how from thenceforth they shall redress this matter with their hands.

Source: J. Brewer, J. Gairdner and J. Brodie, *Letters and papers, foreign and domestic of the reign of Henry VIII*, 1509–47 vol. II, London, 1862–1910, quoted in Denys Cook, *The sixteenth century, documents and debates*, Basingstoke, 1996, p. 24

2.4 Justices of the peace and jury panels

An Act against Perjury, Unlawful Maintenance and Corruption in Officers, 1495

The king, our sovereign lord, well understanding the heinous and detestable perjuries daily committed within this realm in inquests and juries . . . the which perjury groweth by unlawful retainders [retainers], maintenance, embracing . . . as well of the sheriffs as of other officers, notwithstanding any laws before this time made for the punishment of such offenders . . . that the justices of the peace . . . admit nor take any panel of such inquests to be returned afore them, but if the same panel be first seen before them, and they reform it by their discretion if cause be.

Source: *The statutes of the realm*, vol. II, p. 589, London, 1817, in R. Lockyer, *Henry VII*, London, 1990, pp. 91–92

Document case-study questions

1 What do 2.1 and 2.2 tell us about how and why Henry VII used bonds and recognisances to restrain the nobility?

2 What does 2.3 tell us about early Tudor sheriffs and about the role of justices of the peace?

3 What does the style and tone of 2.4 tell us about Wolsey's administration of law and order for Henry VIII?

4 Describe the function of 'retainders' in 2.4. What were the intentions of the Acts of Livery and Maintenance?

Notes and references

1 See R. Lockyer, *Henry VII*, pp. 88–89, London; Denys Cook, *The sixteenth century, documents and debates*, Basingstoke, 1980; and Document 2.3 for the Star Chamber under Wolsey.

2 Penry Williams, 'The crown and the counties', in Christopher Haigh, (ed.), *The reign of Elizabeth I*, London, 1984, pp. 137–38 and pp. 126–27.

3 See Lockyer, *Henry VII*, pp. 26–27 and pp. 86–87.

4 See especially, Keith Wrightson's essay, 'The politics of the parish in early modern England', in Paul Griffiths, Adam Fox and Steve Hindle (eds.), *The experience of authority in early modern England*, Basingstoke, 1996, pp. 9–46.

5 See M. Spufford, 'Puritanism and social control', in A. Fletcher and J. Stevenson (eds.), *Order and disorder in early modern England*, Cambridge, 1985.

6 For pre-Reformation parliaments see Michael Graves, *Elizabethan parliaments, 1559–1601*, London, 1987, pp. 1–7; J. A. F. Thompson, *The transformation of medieval England, 1370–1529*, pp. 273–83; and Lockyer, *Henry VII*, pp. 41–52.

3 The church, religion and authority

The impact of the church on society

The level of authority and influence wielded by the church is perhaps the most vexed question in the entire period. Even when scrutinising the fifteenth century it is difficult to pronounce unequivocally upon the church's impact upon society and politics. Although nominally Catholic, and a contented realm within Christendom, fifteenth-century England was home to the remnants of a home-grown heresy, Lollardy, whose survival, despite persecution, is attested as late as 1516 by the convolutions of the Hunne case.[1] It was a realm, furthermore, that was subject to the same dismal catalogue of clerical failings as any within Christendom. Even a cursory glance at the writings of Sir Thomas More or of Simon Fish highlights a familiar chronicle of worldly priests, apathetic nuns, drunken and idle monks and avaricious prelates. Indeed, until 1529, Cardinal Wolsey displayed a full hand of sins in his own person and career, combining nepotism, non-residence, simony, extravagance, politicking and unchastity. Such faults could not fail to undermine the prestige and moral power of church personnel at all levels of society.

It is also true that the two kings, Henry VI and Richard III, who both at times displayed unusual and emotional piety and loyalty to the late-medieval church, represented in their very different ways a total unsuitability for the role of king. Neither were likely to attract admirers through their piety, given the disasters of their reigns. However, two more successful monarchs, Edward IV and Henry VII, were no more than conventionally pious and did little or nothing either to aid or to impede the church. Given that Wolsey was half-hearted in his resistance to the advance of Lutheranism in the 1520s, the progressive decay of the English church was allowed to proceed largely undisturbed until the king's Great Matter decreed otherwise in 1529. This does not mean that Protestant Reformation was either inevitable or even likely had Henry's marital problems not intervened. Given the career of Cardinal Reginald Pole, who started a systematic and effective reform of the English Catholic church in Mary's reign, and the general progress of the Catholic Reformation in the mid-sixteenth century, it is arguable that the English church was as redeemable as those of Spain, Italy and southern Germany. Nevertheless, the authority of the church, the inviolability of its property and the respect accorded its personnel were undoubtedly at a low ebb at all levels in England from the Wars of the Roses through to 1529. At this point the regime and parliament criticised the church, appropriated its property and questioned its beliefs.

The church, law and government

The church possessed its own courts and exercised its own system of law, canon law. Its priests were subject to canon law (benefit of clergy), its clerics and pensioners subject to its pronouncements upon morality and good order and to its sanctions. To a large extent, this moral sway reinforced good order and contributed towards the peace of the kingdom. However, venality and even criminality among its priests at any level not only undermined good order but under benefit of clergy might mock the law of the land itself. Kings increasingly set benefit and sanctuary aside, whether in the form of Richard III persuading his nephew out of sanctuary and into the Tower for his murderous purposes, or in the form of Henry VIII's new Treasons Act which argued that treason was too heinous a crime to admit of sanctuary or benefit. Furthermore, the 1393 Statute of Praemunire had long been used to limit the legal jurisdiction of the papacy within the realm. Since the quarrels of Henry II, and of King John with the papacy, there had been a traditional wariness of the papal power in England.

The church, represented by Convocation, and with its prelates and senior abbots in the House of Lords, was consulted by the crown and was used to negotiating over its wealth and its financial contributions to the realm. The *Valor Ecclesiasticus* drawn up by Cromwell from 1535 was not part of a new procedure. For that matter, fines levied by Henry VIII from 1530 to 1531 were not unlike the various forced loans and contributions solicited by earlier monarchs.

Furthermore, the church, through its courts and its priestly training traditionally provided the most likely avenue for ambitious and able figures to progress into government posts. As noted earlier, the councils and key administrative posts of the earlier Tudors were dominated by able clerics such as Morton, Warham, Fox and Wolsey. Even More and Cromwell began their administrative careers in clerical households. Yet the church was vulnerable.

The Reformation

Different interpretations

Three views of the origins and course of the English Reformation have emerged over the years. A. G. Dickens argued at length and in detail that the Reformation was a 'bottom-up' process driven by a number of humble and middle-class activists and converts.[2] Others have put forward a 'top-down' process in which Henry VIII, Cranmer and Cromwell were able to impose a settlement that was then driven on by radicals of the mid-Tudor period and consolidated, after the 'blip' of the Marian period, by the Elizabethan Church Settlement. A recent biography of Thomas Cranmer strikingly advances this view, with its detailed picture of the struggles of Cranmer in alliance with his evangelists (enthusiastic Protestants) to contain and rescue the firebrands while tackling the implacable conservatives in the royal council.[3] An extreme revisionist view from the Catholic historian, J. J. Scarisbrick, backed in part by E. Duffy and Christopher Haigh, suggests that Protestant conversion, if it genuinely occurred at all, was late and slow.[4] Where Scarisbrick details the careful preservation of Catholic rituals and relics for decades after the break, Haigh pointedly 'questions the validity of a Protestant-based and critical approach to the late medieval church', while Duffy attests to the 'intrinsic interest and vitality of fifteenth-century and early-sixteenth-century English Catholicism'. Moreover, in relation to specific village communities, he suggests that, 'nothing irreversible had happened by 1554, and the patterns of Catholic devotion readily and rapidly reasserted themselves'.

Given the Erastian nature of the Tudor monarchs' approach to the Church of England, whereby they held that it was subject to the control and direction of the head of state, and, for that matter, the profoundly authoritarian attitudes of both Lutheran and Calvinist reformers, one is inclined to sympathise with the top-down viewpoint. High politics and concern for the succession strongly influenced the religious settlements of Henry VIII and of all three of his children. Above all, both Henry and Elizabeth were, at all times, concerned less with doctrine than with the security and stability of the state. Their success in maintaining such stability in contrast to the disastrous events in Edward's and Mary's reigns, underlines their justified caution when dealing with religious extremes. If anything, the zeal of Edward and Mary equally profoundly exemplified the dangers of excessive religious commitment.

Nevertheless, Henry was seizing a moment and flowing with a tide of religious and intellectual opinion, most obvious among the educated class. Yet that alone cannot explain the humbler martyrs of Smithfield under Mary, nor the rise of what became known as puritanism. It is difficult also to ignore the genuinely reformist, deeply held and rapidly developing opinions of Henry's most active ministers, Cranmer and Cromwell. Both were consummate politicians, but both were utilising political means to secure spiritual ends. Moreover, their opinions and actions found ready support from a wide spectrum of courtiers, nobles, administrators and gentry, including figures such as Norfolk, Gardiner, Wriothesley and Audley. They materially and politically benefited from the break with Rome and the looting of the church and yet were to count themselves among the conservative opposition later on in the Reformation. Henry himself, of all people, was to be found in the Six Articles debates and in the *King's book*, and perhaps consciously in his rejection of the Cleves marriage and his wedding to Catherine Howard, placing himself among the ranks of the conservative opposition. These names and actions strongly suggest an array of base, material and political motives at work. The break with Rome and the dissolutions had deep religious implications, but they provided Henry with several very practical advantages in money and power. His courtiers stood to benefit likewise.

Money and power

Up to perhaps 1535 or 1536, the Reformation provided significant benefits to several different and powerful cliques at court without necessarily involving too many profound spiritual complications. While idealists such as Fisher and More paid with their offices and their lives for their principled opposition to the

A print engraved in Rome showing the hanging and disembowelling of the Carthusians in 1535 for denying the Royal Supremacy. Brutal punishment was meted out against outsiders, whether conservatives, heretics, witches or rogues. In what ways did heresy, witchcraft and vagrancy represent new challenges to good order?

religious and political changes, gentlemen clerks and lawyers such as Rich and Audley, magnates such as Norfolk, and great churchmen such as Bishop Gardiner, went with the tide, took the requisite oaths and prospered. Religion was inevitably taken up by faction politics and the sway of Henry's marital affairs. Apparently principled opponents to Cranmer's and Cromwell's reforms and their spiritual implications also sought to checkmate the reformers' political influence and re-establish the conservatives' hold on good old money and power. This could be very bloody. Again, Diarmaid MacCulloch in his portrait of Cranmer tells of the cold-blooded sacrifice of conservative and evangelical priests to trial and execution (often by burning) which marked the ebb and flow of Cranmer's and his enemies' influence. Whatever the spiritual doctrines at stake, by 1529, the authority, respect and status enjoyed by the late-medieval church was insufficient to save it from a political coup which was led by Henry and his advisers and supported by moderate or areligious figures among court, parliament, nobility and gentry. They plundered the church for its wealth and its land, the return of which, even under Mary, was never remotely feasible. If money and power underlies authority, this aspect of the English Reformation saw an irreversible shift from the church to secular forces. These ranged from the greatest of magnates, to the lawyers and 'new men' who physically carried through the process, and ultimately through the classes represented in the House of Commons, down to the yeomanry. Their successful acquisition of additional wealth and increased status was arguably the culmination of a dynamic process which preceded the break with Rome. In other words, economic, social and political changes had earlier created the momentum by which a declining clergy was in no position successfully to resist a prospering secular educated class. It is a cliché to talk about the rising gentry (and of course their risen and rising noble betters), but, like all clichés, there is a great deal of truth in this one.

Class and region

Before examining less formal aspects of authority in sixteenth-century England, it is worth discussing some of the details regarding religious changes. It is clear that the church's vulnerability was not merely one of morality or theology. Its wealth was a target as was its function as a social, political and spiritual institution. In other words, it could not defend its relative independence as a papal institution within the kingdom of England, nor its privileges, nor its wealth. Neither Henry, nor parliament was willing any longer to tolerate its rivalry. Yet there is overwhelming evidence that refutes any simple 'top-down' explanation for the English Reformation. Much of this evidence is regional. Stated simply, Protestantism and change were welcomed in the south and east of the country, while most, though not all resistance to the Reformation manifested itself in the north and west. This was a pattern that endured into and throughout the English Civil War.

The reasons for some of these regional differences are obvious. Kent, Sussex and London were in proximity to the Channel ports and exposed to floods of printed propaganda from the Protestant reformers on the Continent; remote regions were not so vulnerable. Physically and politically the great estates of Northumberland and Westmorland functioned as distantly removed and semi-detached parts of the kingdom. Moreover, there is plentiful evidence from the Pilgrimage of Grace in the economically depressed North and in the Cornish Rebellion of 1549 that various aspects of the old religion were still well appreciated, particularly among the ignorant commons. The dissolution of the monastic houses, for instance, and the loss of their charitable functions had a practical impact in the North that impinged upon the common people rather more than it had in the south of the country. Likewise, the Cornish people were hardly alone in deriving comfort and certainty from the familiar Latin drones of the old service, while being alarmed by a Prayer Book written in a metropolitan English vernacular that they may have found difficult to understand.

One hesitates to pronounce Protestantism's appeal as an urban phenomenon, yet its success in London parallels similar success in the prosperous towns and cities of northern Germany, and the thriving ports of the Netherlands. Large and crowded populations, higher literacy, proximity of printing presses, difficulty of suppression all favoured urban heresy where remoteness, illiteracy, rural tradition and conservatism could work against it. Ironically, the history of medieval heresy, with the outstanding example of the Cathars of southern France and northern Spain in the fourteenth century, suggests that in earlier times the opposite was the case. Formerly, it was remote and mountainous regions that favoured both heresy and alleged witchcraft for the simple reason that authority found it difficult to reach and suppress outbreaks of unorthodox worship.[5] In the English Reformation, however, it tended to be the government that was heretical and the opposition that was remote.

The attitude of the government to dissent

Governments differed in their treatment of the religiously defiant depending upon the rank of the offenders within society. Thus, the common supporters of the Pilgrimage of Grace and of the Northern Rebellion of 1569 paid in large numbers with their lives for their challenge to the regime. Likewise, Henry VIII's exemplary executions of heretics and of over-zealous Catholics tended to be drawn from the lower reaches of society. More and Fisher died only after every effort had been made to coerce or wheedle them into highly publicised and high-ranking submission to the regime. Troublemakers such as Anne Askew, Elizabeth Barton and Robert Aske were simultaneously too lowly and too prominent to be allowed to prosper in their defiance of the regime.[6] Similarly, Mary carefully avoided direct persecution of Protestants of high social rank. Plenty of time was afforded to allow gentlemen of tender consciences to retire to the country or the continent, safe from the executioner's flames. Yet defiance among the lower ranks had to be rooted out by brutal example. It may be argued that Mary's treatment of the Oxford Martyrs, and the killings of two would-be recanters of their heresies, Northumberland and Cranmer, oppose this argument. However, Latimer and Ridley, who died together in Oxford, had specifically failed to submit to the Catholic regime, and had failed discreetly to retire, to remain silent or to exile themselves. They represented a dangerous example to the lower ranks.

Meanwhile, Northumberland and Cranmer were personally delinquent to Mary. Their recantations were welcome, were potentially useful but were in some ways irrelevant. Both had sought to change the succession at Mary's expense, and meddle in the highest question of political authority in the land. Northumberland had set up the whole Lady Jane Grey episode, while Cranmer had persecuted Mary's mother and had declared Mary to be illegitimate. It was these deeds that probably doomed them, while Mary and her religious adherents showed particular vindictiveness in prescribing the flames for Cranmer even when he had recanted. Cranmer's final heroic withdrawal of his recantation was a matter of proud rejection of the humiliations the Marians sought to impose upon him in public. He was already doomed to burn at the stake.[7]

Political submission to due authority was all, hence the unlikely survival of the young Catholic duke of Norfolk in Elizabeth's reign. Only his persistent foolishness forced his elimination. The chief Catholic victims of Elizabeth's reign were not the long-established and largely quiescent families of old believers. The regime, rather, cracked down on the missionaries and Jesuits, the plotters and conspirators who were perceived more in terms of the defence of the realm than of its religion.

What later became known as 'occasional conformity' became an important aspect of life under the Elizabethan government. Prominent and humble Catholics often found it advisable to take Communion occasionally in order to avoid punishment under the recusancy laws, or to maintain acceptability for office.

On the other side of the religious divide, it was the political challenge over the succession and over parliamentary pretensions that condemned Protestant zealots such as Wentworth and Stubbs to imprisonment or mutilation. Meanwhile, mockery, defiance and embarrassment of the regime and, in particular, of the episcopate which by 1588 had become a major prop of the regime, also brought lethal revenge down on the heads of the puritans suspected of printing the scurrilous anti-episcopal Marprelate tracts.[8]

Such attitudes reflect the importance of legitimate authority in dealing with religious attitudes. Martin Luther embodied the dilemma for reformers in his pamphlet denouncing the 'hordes of murderous thieving peasants' who had been unleashed in Germany in the 1520s through their 'misinterpretation' of Luther's doctrines. Luther detested the peasants and the knights who had, in separate rebellions, questioned due authority and cited his theories in justification. He urged merciless punishment of these miscreants, while steadfastly remaining absolutely reliant upon the protection and support of the Protestant princes of northern Germany, who represented the civil power against whom the peasants and knights had been fighting. Luther stressed the absolute authority of the civil power.

A similar attitude underpinned Henry VIII's fear that vernacular scripture and prayer would, in the hands of women and commoners, upset and challenge due authority. The excessive tolerance of social and religious nonconformity and unrest during Edward VI's reign was shortlived and was loudly condemned by the upper ranks of society to be dangerously subversive of all authority, rank and order.

To sum up, if the English Reformation was to some extent a 'bottom-up' phenomenon, the upper ranks of society were careful to squash undue enthusiasm and unrest among the commoners and were swift to eliminate rebels, traitors, priests and even ministers who meddled with the succession, or stirred up dangerous religious zeal. Where possible, the great ones used different aspects of the Reformation to reinforce their wealth and power.

The fall of Wolsey and the fate of Henry's servants

3.1 Cardinal Wolsey

George Cavendish, in his biography of Wolsey, describes his appearance

He would issue out apparelled all in red, in the habit of a cardinal . . . the best that money could buy. And upon his head a round pillion, with a neck of black velvet . . . he had also a tippet of fine sables around his neck.

There was also borne before him, first the Great Seal of England, and then his cardinal's hat, by a nobleman or some worthy gentleman, with two great crosses of silver borne before him: with also two great pillars of silver . . . and thus he went until he came to Westminster Hall door.

Source: George Cavendish, *The life and death of Cardinal Wolsey*, ed. by R. S. Sylvester, Oxford, 1959, in Denys Cook (ed.), *The sixteenth century, documents and debates*, Basingstoke, 1980, pp. 23–24

3.2 The Cardinal's fall

The fall of Wolsey as described by a modern historian

Wolsey's fall was sudden and total . . . [his] eminence had been lonely, and his fall left him almost totally deserted. Many of his servants hastened to seek other employment, and the leading members of his household entered the King's service.

Source: G. R. Elton, *Reform and Reformation*, London, 1977, pp. 111–12

3.3 Sir Thomas More's downfall

Sir Thomas More in conversation with his son-in-law, William Roper

I find his grace my very good lord indeed, and I believe he doth as singularly favour me as any subject within this realm. Howbeit . . . may tell thee I have no cause to be proud thereof, for if my head could win him a castle in France, it should not fail to go.

Source: William Roper, *The Lyfe of Sir Thomas Moore Knight*, 1515, ed. by E. V. Hitchock, London, 1935, pp. 20–21

3.4 The fall of Thomas Cromwell

A modern historian, G. R. Elton, comments on the fate of Cromwell

It was too late. Allegedly he [Cromwell] planned to lay hold of others among the men arrayed against him, but before he could get Henry's compliance Norfolk and Gardiner finally broke through . . . he was himself arrested at the Council table . . . And so he passed into the Tower, whither he had sent so many men and women, never to leave it. His goods were seized at once, a fatally conclusive sign.

Source: G. R. Elton, *Reform and Reformation*, London, 1977, pp. 291–92

1 What does 3.1 tell you about why there was resentment about the pomp and expense of Wolsey's court? How far do you think Wolsey's display and conceit was justified?

2 What do the circumstances of Wolsey's fall in 3.2 tell us about the nature of power in the 1520s?

3 Compare and contrast Cromwell's fall in 3.4 with that of Wolsey in 3.2. What do these passages tell us about the king and about faction?

4 What does Thomas More's remark in 3.3 about a castle in France and the fate of Wolsey and Cromwell in 3.2 and 3.4 tell us about royal power and royal favour?

Notes and references

1 Richard Hunne was imprisoned by the church courts, allegedly committing suicide by hanging in his cell in 1514. His corpse was burnt under condemnation of heresy as a Lollard. See G. R. Elton, *Reform and Reformation*, London, 1977, pp. 51–53.

2 A. G. Dickens, *The English Reformation*, London, 1964, stresses the continuity between Lollardy and Lutheranism, the importance of pre-Reformation literature, and the effect of printing and preaching upon the grassroots.

3 D. MacCulloch, *Thomas Cranmer*, London, 1996.

4 J. J. Scarisbrick, *The English Reformation and the English people*, Oxford, 1984; E. Duffy, *The stripping of the altars: traditional religion in England, 1450–1580*, New Haven, 1992; Christopher Haigh (ed.), *The English Reformation*, Cambridge, 1987.

5 Emmanuel Roy Ladurie, *Montaillou*, London, 1978; and Hugh Trevor-Roper, *The European witch-craze of the sixteenth and seventeenth centuries*, London, 1969.

6 Elizabeth Barton, otherwise known as the Nun of Kent, had seen visions, denounced the royal divorce and was executed for treason in 1534, see Elton, *Reform and Reformation*, pp. 180–82. Anne Askew was active in the 1540s as a notorious heretic and preacher. She was burned to death in 1546, see Dickens, *English Reformation*, pp. 269–70.

7 For a full and moving account of this episode, see MacCulloch, *Cranmer*.

8 The Marprelate Tracts were a series of savage pamphlet attacks by puritan groups associated with the Barrowists (an extreme group of puritan reformers led by John Barrow and active in the late 1580s and early 1590s) upon the Elizabethan Church Settlement in general and upon the bishops in particular. Published in the late 1580s, they ceased after the execution of the Barrowists.

4 'The great web' – informal authority

Society in disarray

Did religious change undermine the natural order of society and the obedience and deference of the lower ranks towards the upper ranks of society? Or were the religious changes one result of demographic and economic developments arising out of overpopulation and plague dating back to the fourteenth century?

However we examine the web of formal and informal relationships which made up society in early modern England, we can see that great changes had taken place and were taking place which threw any assumptions of a static and structured order of society into disarray. Sumptuary laws, dating back to the Middle Ages, and contemporary Statutes of Artificers and repeated official Poor Laws all sought to establish and maintain wage rates and limits, rules and gradations for skilled and unskilled workers and apprentices. Yet economic depression, soaring inflation, labour gluts and shortages, wars and famines rendered such attempts futile.

At times, indigence and vagrancy created an angry and mobile population of the dispossessed, who could not, it seemed, be contained within the existing boundaries of parish control. There were plenty of sturdy recruits available for the frequent rebellions of the Tudor period. Moreover, authorities at county and parish level were familiar with an ever present threat that an armed riot could easily be provoked by hunger and deprivation. Yet the historian, John Beattie, has suggested that there took place 'a very long-term transformation of the place of violence in English society, from a period in the Middle Ages when violence was less restrained either by the state or by men's attitudes, to what has come to be the broad disapproval and control of private violence in the modern world'.[1]

Much of this change was in place by the early-seventeenth century, with a great deal of it due to specific changes in law and formal authority at central and local level. However, much was equally due to informal controls within families, parishes and congregations. In an era of profound economic, religious and social change, what men perceived as moral and acceptable in conducting and maintaining normal everyday activities and relationships with family members, neighbours, colleagues, social inferiors and superiors was an essential part of the story of order and disorder. Paradoxically, different ways of disciplining society would include not less but more formal disciplinary violence, sometimes carefully limited in the form of teachers and fathers beating their charges, or the parish beating the vagrant, or expanded in scope, where the state tortured and executed traitors. Control of violence was all.

A male-dominated society

In essence, England was and remained a severely male-dominated or patriarchal society throughout the Tudor period and for a long time afterwards. Substantial work by Lawrence Stone over nearly a quarter of a century, covering the family, sex, marriage and divorce from the early modern period onwards, ultimately confirms the essential chauvinism which dominated all aspects of society.

As with the family, so with the state, there was a pronounced dislike of the notion of female government which disrupted the politics not only of England, but those of the neighbouring kingdoms of France and Scotland to a very significant degree in the sixteenth century. There was, of course, a difference between theory and practice at all levels of society, as Bernard Capp has illustrated in his account of women and authority. He bears witness to the exceptions, such as Bess of Hardwicke, who wielded real local power, to the existence in practical terms of matriarchy, and even to the phenomenon of 'disorderly women' on a substantial and riotous level.[2]

Thus, the 'monstrous regimen of women', famously detested by John Knox, included a formidable trio of powerful women sovereigns in Mary of Guise, Catherine de Medici and Mary Queen of Scots, while, to his embarrassment, Knox was soon confronted by the phenomenon that was Elizabeth I.

It has been remarked that 'no consensus has yet emerged on the long-term changes in women's position over this period as a whole'. Capp argues that for historians and for contemporaries three positions emerged. Women were submissive, accommodating or defiant. It would seem that the least dignified, that of uncomplicated submission in a brutally male world, was a standard and sensible policy for most females for most of the time. Real and wide-ranging change in status would await the practical efforts of sympathetic Victorian men such as John Stuart Mill and W. E. Gladstone, three centuries on.

Strong women and moral panic

Nevertheless, accidents of mortality and circumstance meant that perhaps 20 per cent of households were headed by women, widows and heiresses being the most obvious exceptions to masculine domination. Examples, not least in Shakespeare, abounded of popular awareness of shrews – unruly and authoritative women. Moreover, community punishment and ostracism of delinquent women were commonplace and seem to have enjoyed fairly solid community support throughout the period. Overall, such opinion seems to have been male-driven, generally accepted, and the shrewish and bossy exceptions who thrived were seen very much as (often humorous) exceptions to the rule.

There is some interesting evidence, too, of unusual male sensitivity to female unruliness and independence, even a degree of 'moral panic' in the late-sixteenth century. This again can perhaps be seen reflected in contemporary literature and humour. In a time of rapid change in many of the cherished certainties of society this was inevitable. Yet prominent women of the age tended still to be widows, heiresses, queens and the very occasional bluestocking.

Marriage

The upper classes

Different conventions affected the upper and lower classes and males and females. It is a commonplace that kings were different from everyone else. A monarch who did not keep mistresses was regarded as odd in the extreme. In some ways, for instance, the amours of the notoriously attractive Edward IV contributed to his aura of kingliness. Morality at court, whether under Henry VIII or Elizabeth I, let alone the boozy, homosexual James I, tended to be notoriously lax, although Elizabeth policed her ladies in waiting and her male favourites with considerable rigour. But this seems to have been as much about preventing wildly unsuitable or personally irritating marriages as reducing promiscuity. However, whereas kings might stray without censure, Mary and Elizabeth, not least by personal inclination, were careful to restrict or eliminate amatory behaviour outside official nuptial diplomacy or negotiation. Genuine or, in Anne Boleyn's case, alleged promiscuity from a queen consort or lady in waiting could lead at best to exile, and at worst to the block.

Double standards also operated for the clergy. It was again a commonplace for a cardinal or bishop to keep a mistress. The Reformation legitimised many an existing relationship between priest and wife.

Commoners

As Lawrence Stone makes clear, divorce of any sort was only an option for noble, rich or powerful males. Marriage, indeed, with few exceptions, remained a material and dynastic contract within affluent and noble families. Where property was lacking, marriage, if entered into at all, was much delayed. Below the rank of yeoman, full and legal marriage was an expensive and unusual luxury. Partnerships were maintained through informal vows, and divorce replaced by simple parting, abandonment or even, up to the early-nineteenth century, by wife sale (often mutually agreed between partners).[3] Formal marriage, when it did occur, came late, as partners or individual males waited on the deaths of parents and the inheritance of a household for sufficient means to set up a household.

Morality and authority

Before the Reformation, the confessional and the rituals associated with penance and forgiveness provided solace for, and discipline of, sinners at all levels of society. Conventional piety could even allow a pious individual to commit all manner of apparently murderous and carnal acts with a clear conscience. At village level the church provided a familiar and comforting set of rituals that enforced basic social discipline without demanding excessive religiosity. A good picture of social norms among commoners in the late medieval period can be found among the Cathar heretics depicted in Ladurie's *Montaillou*,[4] in which heretics and conventional Catholics alike reconciled periods of minor promiscuity with equalled unemphatic chastity. Although allowance needs to be made for the remote mountainous location of the Montaillou community, this picture of restraint nevertheless rings true for most of peasant Christendom. The church and religion provided ground rules bolstered by neighbourhood sanctions against extremes of behaviour. More formal constraints became important further up the social scale, where any kind of marriage became a property transaction, rules of inheritance mattered, and adultery or promiscuity, unless tolerated within careful limits, became dangerous. This was because of the implicit threat posed to the network of property and power agreements set by marriage among the great families.

The higher in society, the more important the marriage agreement. Authority became severely intolerant of ill-chosen alliances and affairs.

Henry VIII's personal life provides some useful examples. Firstly, his marriage to Catherine of Aragon highlighted his father's anxiety not to lose the benefits of her original marriage to Henry's brother Arthur, which were threatened by Arthur's premature death. Secondly, in later life, Anne Boleyn's and Catherine Howard's melancholy fates marked the terrible dangers faced by high-born women should they succumb to temptation or even suspicion of temptation before and after marriage. The young princess Elizabeth, likewise, took appalling risks in her adolescent flirtations with Thomas Seymour, the Lord High Admiral and third husband of Catherine Parr.

Later, we find Elizabeth directing the amours and alliances of her courtiers with painstaking care and frequent severity. Much of this was personal, as in her furious interest in the personal life of her favourite, Robert Dudley, while her treatment of erring ladies in waiting and senior courtiers demonstrated a minute sensitivity to what was and what was not acceptable. Promiscuous or embarrassingly fertile affairs, such as those of Ann Vavasour (with the earl of Oxford), Elizabeth Throckmorton (with Sir Walter Ralegh), and of Frances Howard to the earl of Hertford, all provoked violence or imprisonment.

That personal relationships between the great inevitably involved money and power was an important truth at this time. Such matters, moreover, became complicated by two other developments which had far-reaching effects. The first, from the 1490s onwards, was the rise of the venereal disease, syphilis. Its symptoms in the first decades of its appearance in Europe were so savage as to affect attitudes towards morality and sexual activity very deeply indeed. The new and terrible disease proved an invaluable ally to the second development – reformed religion.

The family

Patriarchy

Put simply, the family unit seems to have become vastly more important in Britain as a result of the Reformation. To quote Lawrence Stone, 'in a society almost entirely without a police force, it was a most valuable institution for social control at village level'.[5]

By the end of the century, a commonplace picture was built up of a middle-class model within which patriarchy was reinforced, with the male head of the family taking over much of the role of the local priest. He led the family in prayers and provided final recourse as arbiter of morals and dispenser of orthodox religious belief. This was certainly a model towards which so-called puritan households aspired, and is, as a cliché, perfectly recognised as a model through Victorian and well into Edwardian times.

The subordinate role of women

The poet Milton summed up his relative view of the sexes with a certain lack of compromise: 'He for God only, she for God in him.' One bishop, Aylmer, went further. For him, one type of woman had made a distinct impression as 'foolish, wanton, flibbeygibs, tattlers, triflers, wavering, witless, without council, feeble, careless, rash, proud, dainty, tale-bearers, eves-droppers, rumour-raisers, evil-tongued, worse minded, and in every way doltified with the dregs of the Devil's dunghill'.[6] To be fair, he also picked out a virtuous type of female but this does show what Elizabeth I had to combat in contemporary male attitudes.

Also, of course, Aylmer's tirade reminds one of the accusations commonly made against suspected witches in this era. Perhaps there was a genuine crisis of the sexes at work. If so, it was not credibly the result of any significant assertion of women's rights. Despite the accidents of birth that put women on the thrones of France, England and Scotland in 1560, examples of educated or powerful women outside widowhood, or a household as extraordinary as that of Sir Thomas More, were rare indeed. Yet women seem to have caused a 'fear of impending breakdown of the social order'.

We know from the number of hanged witches where some of this fear led. At village level there is plentiful evidence, not only in the witch-craze, but in the use of the scold's bridle, rough music, ducking stools and the clowning and abuse of charivari, of a brutal enthusiasm for communal self-help that was directed at certain clear targets. One was the witch, but the scold, the faithless wife, the single mother and the whore also attracted much attention.

Violence and discipline

Adolescents and beggars

Violence and communal disgrace were not always gender-specific, however, for the sturdy and the less than sturdy beggar also attracted both legislation and physical manhandling. Moreover, there was a distinct assumption around the country, arising partly from the undoubted fact of a buoyant population, that 'adolescents and youths were seen by many as primary instigators of disorder'.[7]

As Robin Briggs points out, in later-sixteenth-century England something like 35 per cent of the population was under the age of 15 and perhaps 54 per cent under 25.[8] That represented a lot of youthful energy to be controlled.

Paul Griffiths has picked out the particular case history of early-modern Norwich to highlight certain aspects of the problem of masterless young people. He points out that their plight was connected with 'a broader concern with social discipline and included the closer policing of alehouses, deeper poverty, begging and inmates',[9] all themes which resonate throughout the chapters of this book.

Griffiths suggests that much trouble, including the increasing lack of stability and security within domestic service, an important employer of young people, derived from the difficulty encountered by growing towns to absorb the drift of the workless from the countryside. As we have already seen, the ups and downs of the sixteenth-century economy virtually guaranteed such instability. To this, youth brought numbers and energy. Characteristically, authorities responded with a similar policy mix at local and national level: discipline, coercion and the moral imperative to work.

Stone's views on the brutality of the contemporary population throw a degree of light upon the upbringing and treatment of the young as well as of the dissident in general, given the relish with which many communal punishments were administered. He describes a society 'in which a majority of the individuals that composed it found it very difficult to establish close emotional ties to any other person'.[10] Stone's explanation – that the majority of children spent their infancy put out to wet-nursing and into the remoteness of stifling swaddling clothes followed by systematic beating as they grew older – is best left to the psychiatrists. A single famous example is that of Henry VIII's ability to swing from genuine uxorious and passionate love to judicial murder in a sequence of love and dynastic matches. This suggests an almost alien approach to emotion and to one's fellow human beings which should be taken into account when looking at these matters of social relationships and reactions. But this does not mean that at all levels children were unloved. Briggs, on the contrary, argues that 'children were the objects of affection and concern to the vast majority of parents . . . in many ways this was a child-centred society'.

Thrashing and good order

In such confines and under such pressures, violence was a popular option, but it was ordered violence as suggested earlier. The role of the patriarch was enhanced. The father within his household was 'priest-ruler' of his tiny empire. Within this 'empire' certain changes worked or were made to work in the man's favour. Printing and the new knowledge, and the end of the church's monopoly on education, if anything widened the educational gap between the male, affluent and educated, on the one hand, and women and the disadvantaged, on the other. Meanwhile, education and upbringing was itself consciously inclined to use brutal means, like the regular beating of women and children, precisely to break the spirit and achieve good order.

In other words, there were perceived threats to good order at work throughout the sixteenth century: evidence of male unease at women's role within society and an awareness of the turbulent throng of young people, male and female, whose hormonally charged potential for misbehaviour needed to be channelled or suppressed. Shakespeare's *King Lear* graphically depicted the horrors of this world as the mad king himself scorned 'the rascally beadle' as he thrashes a whore, and sees humanity 'at it pell mell'. The images are striking in picking out almost orgiastic sexual activity and overactivity, entwined with hierarchies of incessant violence. Significantly, in a hierarchical society, each rank assumed, and was entitled to, the right to thrash the next rank down. Schoolmaster thrashed pupil, father thrashed son, daughter and wife, beadle thrashed whore and vagrant, and master thrashed servant.

Master and servant

Within the middle and upper classes there was a revealing relationship – that between master and servant. Masters often beat servants with enthusiasm. The diarist, Samuel Pepys, a genial man, writing in the mid-seventeenth century, gave regular accounts of a relationship of this kind, together with detailed examples of the habitual assumption of sexual advantage taken by master over female servant. There was also the continual assumption of the master's right to oversee the private life and morals of his servants. Strong echoes of this latter assumption can be seen in Elizabeth's treatment of her ladies in waiting mentioned earlier. Interestingly, for the purposes of genteel adultery or intrigue, servants seem to have been classed as unseeing, unfeeling unpersons, who were meant to be oblivious to the personal lives of their employers.

Seen in this light, much social legislation and much of the action regarding poverty, vagrancy and disorder taken during the Tudor years, becomes understandable. At local and national level, law and administrative arrangements were put into place by gentlemen, by masters. These were men who presumed to know the moral needs of an inferior population. That population had to be restrained from disorder, sexual excess, drunkenness and wantonness. They had to be prevented from lapsing into idleness or vagrancy, that is from wandering beyond the reach of their appointed regional sources of authority. Such law-making, law-administering men feared scolds and shrewish women and disapproved of the surplus of adolescent troublemakers. Naturally, the legislation produced and presided over by these Tudor rulers provided for exemplary use of violence in the forms of lashes and mutilation.

As Griffiths points out, household and workplace were crucial in disciplining youth. Norwich magistrates were most worried by those youths and girls who were 'out of hand' or 'out of service'. When neither master nor household was on hand to control young folk, the state or the local magistracy had to step in.

The reformation of manners

Beneath this concern for the behaviour of the single unattached man, or for that matter, the single mother, we find again a concern among the rulers for the morality of the ruled. There was a Tudor concern for the reformation of manners.

Action against prostitution

The later medieval period in Europe, from 1350 to about 1480, has been described as 'the golden age of prostitution'. There are some suggestions that *de facto* toleration of such lechery arose from the demoralisation that accompanied and lingered after the Black Death. Whatever the cause, the English seem to have been anxious to reform behaviour.

Pre-Reformation efforts have been portrayed by historians as spasmodic, localised or poorly sustained.[11] However, recent research suggests that there was a major effort to reform manners and to clamp down on sexual immorality through the Wars of the Roses and into Henry VII's reign. There was an undoubted incentive to act against the immoral as stricter forms of Protestantism became popular, and this, together with other developments in social discipline discussed above, probably fuelled the tendency towards harsher, often physical, punishment for transgressors after 1560.

Feminist interpretation

Given that marriage effectively subordinated wife to husband and deprived her of individual rights under the law, prostitutes, particularly if unmarried, together with widows, represented rogue examples of womenfolk. Just as unmarried mothers were treated with brutal rigour by parish authorities and attracted communal opprobrium, and elderly women were in the majority among the victims of the British witch-craze, so prostitutes attracted increasing hostility from government, community, parish and household. To quote Patricia Crawford, 'When, in practice, women stepped outside the clearly defined boundaries which had been drawn, they challenged fundamental axioms of social life in ways which men found socially subversive and deeply threatening to their sexuality.'[12] Certain figures stand out in the turbulent era of religious change, such as Anne Askew and Elizabeth Barton, both given to visions and public utterance and both executed.

Certain specifically female crimes fell foul of the urge to reform manners. Prostitutes and single mothers suffered severely from the church courts and could expect short shrift from what, for lack of a better word, could be called puritanism. If prostitution was one crime, infanticide was clearly another which seems to have attracted particularly harsh treatment. Anne Laurence claims that this crime made up some 7 per cent of all homicides in sixteenth-century Middlesex and, during the medieval period it constituted a not unexpected or particularly reprehensible 'solution to the problem of an unwanted child'. Less tolerant times were on the way, and the same forces that leaned on the single mother and whipped the adulterer were at work towards the end of the sixteenth century. However, more enlightened views seem to have prevailed, seemingly over the same period as the ruling class gradually relaxed its attitude to witchcraft. Further into the seventeenth century we find infanticide effectively decriminalised with 'a recognition that a newly delivered woman might be in an altered psychological state'.[13]

Class or religion

The large number of cases brought against the morally delinquent in the second half of the sixteenth century gave rise to the suggestion that a puritan elite was at work reforming manners among the lower classes. However, the historian, M. Spufford, has traced such discipline farther back into the thirteenth and fourteenth centuries, and suggests not only that 'theological debate was very lively amongst the humble and not only the village oligarchs in the sixteenth century',[14] but that the enforcement of moral censure predominantly among the poorer classes was simply a reflection of the continued discipline of the poor by the rich.

Doubtless there was a strong element of continuity at work here. Nevertheless, evidence of 'masterless men' at all levels of society, and of a genuine unease at the vagrant, the outspoken individual and those who were not members of a household, suggests that something new and disturbing was going on. It seems that the threat of new forms of subversion and disorder was alarming traditional authority which, among the gentry, received a significant reinforcement in the form of puritan strictness.

The witch-craze

Margaret Murray, in a long discredited study asked, 'Were there really witches?' More recently, James Sharpe has rather complacently declared, 'There were, simply, too many checks and balances in the English system to allow a witch-craze to develop.'[15] Even if one dismisses the slaughter of at least 120 witches by Matthew Hopkin in the 1640s as a distinct aberration from English practice, this view is hard to justify. In addition to Hopkin's victims, there remain the trials and hangings of several hundred old women, most notably in Essex and Scotland, where the number and nature of the proceedings certainly seem to have constituted a distinct witch phenomenon. True, Sharpe points out convincingly that the English judicial system, despite Hopkin, worked eventually to tighten up proof of guilt and sought to reduce innocent loss of life, suggesting a situation existed where, although the majority of the English population accepted the likelihood of witchcraft at work, that majority was alert to the dangers of overcredulity.

Certain aspects of the 'craze' and of the historical debate over its extent and significance stand out. Firstly, it happened and the authorities made significant moves. Elizabeth's government introduced a major statute in 1563 to deal with the problem. Large numbers of elderly women were hanged after denunciations from their neighbours suggesting that they had committed *maleficium* (literally an evil act) against specific members of the community. Such an evil act might constitute a misfortune as trifling as a minor injury or the death of a stock animal, but it might also involve the sickness or even death of a human being. Whatever it was, we can accept that individuals, most notably in Essex villages, felt harmed and blamed old ladies for that sense of harm, with fatal consequences.

Secondly, religious change made a difference. While on the continent there was a thriving campaign against witchcraft and a theology to back it up, in England there was a sense, up to a point, that Catholicism was itself a kind of sorcery. Keith Thomas, in *Religion and the decline of magic*,[16] has made a good case for the survival of Latin tags and Catholic forms in 'white' magic. Likewise, there is evidence that professed witches were often deluded into believing in their own 'black' powers, or were actually dabbling in 'white' magic.

To some extent we can say that the witch-craze was 'a broyle against old women'.[17] It is also clear that sane and intelligent members of the elite, up to and including royalty (notably James I) not only believed in and feared witches but, remarkably, also tolerated very dubious practices among the elite. Notables in Elizabeth's reign such as Walter Ralegh and John Dee escaped serious censure, although their discussions and meetings attracted the attention of the Elizabethan secret service. As with the reformation of manners there is a hint, noted by James Sharpe, that, while the elite escaped, the witch-craze in England affected 'the activities of peasants rather than the intelligent'.[18]

Finally, all the evidence suggests that although the intelligent, albeit often warily, subscribed to witch beliefs, they were effectively acquiescing in and processing witchcraft trials arising from village level, in other words the witch-craze was a 'bottom-up' phenomenon. As such, while it was undoubtedly an aspect of social control, give or take a few elements of hysteria, particularly among elderly 'witches' and their alleged victims, prosecution was virtually forced upon the elite by popular request in order to sooth parish worries and hatreds. Thus, it is perhaps useful to class this singular phenomenon along with the rough music, the mistreatment of the single mother, and the persecution of the scold, as a further compelling example of the way the ruling classes sought to impose 'top-down' solutions for social control. It is also an example of how they were as happy to co-opt commoners and their fears and prejudices at the grassroots in the interests, if not of absolutely good order, at least of less bad disorder. Better, perhaps, a few dead witches and a quiet village.

Poverty and vagrancy

The poor

Something happened to the status of the poor during the Tudor era. A. L. Beier refers to the 'de-sanctification of the poor'.[19] There is a lot of truth in this comment. Medieval Christendom had built up a considerable network of religious and monastic orders, charities, hospitals and alms-givers that derived their *raison d'être* and their self-respect from the relief of poverty and its attendant ills. Given the power of the Franciscan order, with its revival of the monastic ideal of poverty during the twelfth century, the high Middle Ages had seen a tendency to idealise poverty. By the late-fifteenth century, the ideals of the Franciscan, Benedictine and Dominican orders had long been tainted by scandal and disrepute, although northern England, in particular, retained a practical appreciation of the benefits of active monastic charity. Moreover, it can be argued that the medieval poor were truly 'biblical'. Like the sufferers in Christ's parables and miracles, they were leprous, halt, barren, lame and old. The 'new' poor of the sixteenth century could be poor, unemployed or, as likely, underemployed, but they could often be rudely healthy and even physically threatening. It was not so much a question of distinguishing between the deserving and the undeserving poor, although that was an obvious and compelling consideration. The distinction was also made between settled and unsettled poor.

Vagabonds

The population growth of the fourteenth century had seen a huge increase in the size and complexity of the towns and cities, within which 'town air made free'. The break-up of feudal control after the Black Death, and the temporary reduction of population which had hastened the death of feudalism in England, had liberated the poor. The working or employable poor had wandered in search of better paid or more amenable work. As the population again rose, once more bringing crisis levels of physically exuberant but underemployed youth in the sixteenth century, the problem of vagrancy arose, made worse by the simultaneous return to foreign war and the decline of traditional feudal methods of recruitment of troops. During lulls in the many wars of the Tudors, soldiery were released from their obligations many miles away from their parishes and into a fluid job market. All too often, recruits were no longer loyal tenants, as they would have been under feudalism, but the sweepings of the jails, unlikely to be absorbed by the community after hostilities had ceased. The sturdy beggar was born!

Beier states unequivocally that 'the poor unquestionably got poorer between 1500 and 1650'.[20] There is evidence of a baby boom, and again, unquestionably, there was an inflation over this period, with prices rising to considerably outstrip wage rates. Other factors, notably enclosure and engrossing of land, plus, of course, frequent warfare added to dispossession and disruption.

For the ruling classes both poverty and vagrancy posed a number of distinct problems. First and most pressing was one of cost. Relief on the parish was levied upon payers of the poor rate, that is the landholders. Although it was increasingly clear that rulers and property owners were willing to pay out for necessary poor relief, there was an undoubted need to justify what was and what was not necessary and to curtail expense where possible.

Poor Laws and yet more Poor Laws were needed over and above local initiatives to deter vagrants and organise cost reduction. But, above all, another consideration loomed for authority. Poor and vagrant folk, particularly if able-bodied, posed a direct challenge to all good order.

The sin of rebellion

4.1 The Pilgrimage of Grace

The examination of Robert Aske and Lord Darcy, April 1537

The said Aske saith, they had communication together touching the said Acts of Parliament [regarding the Royal Supremacy], and saith by his faith he can not remember now any notorious communication betwixt the Lord Darcy and himself in denial of the authority of the Supreme Head.

Item, if you, my Lord Darcy, had despaired to defend the castle of Pontefract . . . why did you not find some means to come to the King's Grace, or to his army, rather than to tarry and to be sworn to the King's enemies?

Source: J. Brewer, J. Gairdner and R. H. Brodie (eds.), *Letters and papers of Henry VIII*, vol. XII, London, 1862–1910

4.2 Kett's Rebellion

Nicholas Sotherton, a gentleman from East Anglia, comments on contemporary events

They [the rebels] appointed a place of assembly among them in an oaken tree . . . and the Gentlemen they took they brought to the tree of Reformation to be seen of the people to demand what they would do with them: where cried hang him and some kill him . . . and indeed they did press their weapons to kill some of these gentlemen.

Source: Nicholas Sotherton, *The commotion in Norfolk, 1549*, B. L. Harleian, MS 576, quoted in A. Fletcher, *Tudor rebellions*, London, 1983, pp. 123–24

4.3 The rebellious state of the country

William Paget, Secretary of State, to Protector Somerset, 1549 (letter)

Marry, the King's subjects out of all discipline, out of obedience, caring neither for Protector nor King, and much less for any other meane officer. And what is the cause? Your own levity, your softness, your opinion to be good to the poor . . . the foot taketh upon him the part of the head, and the commons is become a king, appointing conditions and laws to the governors.

Source: *Cal. S. P. Domestic Edward VI*, vol. VIII, 4, quoted in A. Fletcher, *Tudor rebellions*, London, 1983, pp. 124–25

4.4 'Certain sermons and homilies appointed by the king's majesty to be declared and read . . . every Sunday', 1547

Exhortation concerning good order and obedience

Almighty God hath created and appointed all things in heaven, earth and waters in a most excellent and perfect order. In heaven he hath appointed distinct orders and states of archangels and angels. In the earth he has assigned King, princes, with other governors under them, all in good and necessary order . . . Every degree of people, in their vocation, calling and office, has appointed to them their duty and order. Some are in high degree, some in low; some kings and princes, some inferiors and subjects, priests and laymen, masters and servants, fathers and children, husbands and wives, rich and poor . . .

Where there is no right order there reigneth all abuse carnal liberty, enormity and babylonical confusion . . . Take away kings, princes, rulers, magistrates, judges and such states of God's order, no man shall ride or go by the highway unrobbed, no man shall sleep in his own house or bed unkilled, no man shall keep his wife, children and possessions in quietness; all things shall be common and there must needs follow all mischief and utter destruction . . .

God hath sent us his high gift, our most dear sovereign Lord, King Edward VI, with godly, wise and honourable council, with other superiors and inferiors, in a beautiful order. Wherefore let us subjects do our bounden duty . . .

Source: G. R. Elton, *The Tudor constitution: documents and commentary*, Cambridge, 2nd edn, 1982, p. 15

Document case-study questions

1 Why was the question put to Lord Darcy in 4.1 a difficult question for him to answer? What does the question tell us of the contract between the king and his nobler subjects?

2 From the evidence in 4.2, how far do you think Kett's Rebellion can be seen as a class conflict aimed at the upper classes?

3 What does Paget's attitude in 4.3 regarding 'softness towards the poor' suggest about likely future policy from Tudor government when faced with discontent among the commons?

4 Compare and contrast Sotherton's views in 4.2 with those expressed in the Homily on obedience in 4.4. What do Sotherton and the Homily tell us about the Tudor ruling class and its views on good order? How important do you think official religion was in maintaining good order?

Notes and references

1 John Beattie, *Crime and the courts in England, 1660–1800*, Oxford, 1986, p. 138, quoted by Steve Hindle in Paul Griffiths, Adam Fox and Steve Hindle (eds.), *The experience of authority in early modern England*, Basingstoke, 1996, p. 227.

2 Bernard Capp, 'Separate domains? women and authority in early modern England', in Griffiths et al., *The experience of authority*, pp. 117–46.

3 Lawrence Stone, *The family, sex and marriage in England, 1500–1800*, London, 1977, p. 37. Wife sale is a feature in the plot of Thomas Hardy's *The Mayor of Casterbridge*.

4 Emmanuel Roy Ladurie, *Montaillou*, London, 1978, pp. 179 ff.

5 Stone, *The family*, p. 27.

6 Milton quoted in Stone, *The family*, p. 154, also Aylmer quoted in the same volume, p. 196.

7 Fletcher and Stevenson, *Order and disorder*, p. 33.

8 Robin Briggs, *Witches and neighbours*, London, 1996, pp. 78–79.

9 Paul Griffiths, 'Masterless young people in Norwich, 1560–1645', in Griffiths et al., *The experience of authority*, pp. 146–87.

10 Stone, *The family*, pp. 98–99.

11 See Griffiths et al., *The experience of authority*, pp. 57–59.

12 Patricia Crawford, *Women and religion in England, 1500–1720*, London, 1993, p. 17.

13 Anne Laurence, *Women in England, 1500–1750*, London, 1994, p. 271.

14 M. Spufford, 'Puritanism and social control', in Fletcher and Stevenson, *Order and disorder*, p. 42.

15 J. A. Sharpe, *Instruments of darkness: witchcraft in England, 1550–1750*, London, 1996, p. 30.

16 Keith Thomas, *Religion and the decline of magic*, London, 1971, is also very strong on white magic and cunning men and women.

17 Quoted regarding the Essex trials in Stuart Clark, *Thinking with demons, the idea of witchcraft in early modern Europe*, Oxford, 1997, p. 75.

18 Sharpe, *Instruments of darkness*, p. 5.

19 A. L. Beier, *Masterless men, the vagrancy problem in England, 1560–1640*, London, 1985, p. 4.

20 A. L. Beier, *The problem of the poor in Tudor and early Stuart England*, London, 1983, p. 7.

5 The mid-Tudor crisis

The root causes of crisis

Although the concept of a mid-Tudor crisis has been much challenged over the last 25 years, it remains a convenient peg upon which to hang a number of important observations on the progress of the Tudor monarchy.

The term 'crisis' can be applied with some vigour to a period in which England was ruled, as has been famously and repeatedly paraphrased, 'by a sick and rapidly ageing bully, a boy too young to rule and a woman of limited political ability'. From 1540 until, perhaps, 1563 England was faced by a series of disastrous foreign wars, four *coups d'état*, three serious rebellions, the rule of the above, plus nine days' worth of a teenage female usurper. It also changed the official state religion perhaps six times, suffered several appalling epidemics in which it lost perhaps a fifth of its population, and was ravaged by economic and financial catastrophe.

It is significant that, throughout these catastrophic challenges, the Tudor state and its administration struggled on, survived and in some respects even thrived. There is an element of truth to G. R. Elton's firm conviction that Thomas Cromwell's alleged 'revolution in government' did have lasting and, in many ways, benign consequences for the Tudor state. Indeed, these years proved the acid test of much that had gone before and, despite her unsuitable sex, at the end of this period the Princess Elizabeth was able to ascend the throne in 1558 and proceed to set her regime upon a firm footing thereafter. Law and order rather than disorder did win through, although it was a close-run thing.

It is arguable that, whatever the horrors of disease, poverty and vagrancy at the bottom of society, we must look at the top for an understanding of the crisis. It was from the top that the principal disputes about the succession, about religion and about local and national authority stemmed.

It is a matter of fact that the period from 1540 to 1560 saw a number of complications involving the succession. Firstly, Henry died before his sickly son, Edward VI, was of age. Thus, despite Henry's best efforts expressed carefully in his will, that will was subverted by the duke of Somerset and the experienced and devious councillor, Paget. When Somerset was himself deposed, his successor, the duke of Northumberland, faced with the imminent prospect of Edward's early death, attempted to exclude the legitimate successors, Mary and Elizabeth, from the throne and place Lady Jane Grey, married to Northumberland's own son, Guildford Dudley, in their stead in 1553. Later, Mary's predicament as both woman and Catholic led her into a controversial marriage with Philip II of Spain. She was desperate to conceive an heir in order to exclude her sister and to retain the throne for a Catholic descendant.

Political change enabled faction to thrive during these years, a process made worse because the business of settling Britain's official religion remained profoundly unsettled when Cromwell was executed in 1540. At first there was a swing in favour of the Catholic and conservative faction led by Bishop Gardiner and the duke of Norfolk. After the disgrace and death of Catherine Howard, there was a stand-off as Henry punished either religious extreme, and came to marry the assuredly Protestant Catherine Parr. The rise of the Seymour brothers and of Dudley, the future duke of Northumberland, might seem to forecast Protestant victory, but the official books and homilies issued by the government suggested otherwise.

So, during Edward's brief reign from 1547 to 1553, there was a distinct lurch towards Protestantism. As the king became older, he became more involved in business and more conspicuously intense in the sincerity and extremity of his own Protestant beliefs. Cranmer, latterly with the inspiration of Zwinglian enthusiasts resident in Britain, put the new religion into words with the first Edwardian Prayer Book of 1549 and the second of 1552. These were backed up by the power of statute in the first and second Acts of Uniformity. Together with the moderation of the heresy and treason laws and the return of clerical marriage, England was, by 1553, at least officially, a Protestant country.

Edward's death, and the failed attempt to settle Lady Jane Grey upon the throne, brought Mary I to power and meant a brief but bloody attempt to restore the Catholic religion. Although Mary's death and her lack of a child thwarted her hopes of Catholic success, nevertheless Elizabeth acceded to the throne in a climate of great uncertainty as to England's religious future.

Meanwhile, society and the economy were in turmoil. The vital cloth trade with the Netherlands was in a state of collapse, harvests were poor, and disease stalked the land. Constant wars with Scotland and France mobilised thousands of troops who were frequently starving, undisciplined and dangerous. The changes in land ownership, the march of enclosure and developments in commercial farming all stirred up a hungry and confused countryside. There was sufficient anger, confusion and despair to provide plentiful recruits for rebellion in 1549 and again in 1554, with unrest becoming endemic in the last years of the unpopular Mary I. Yet somehow, the state defeated rebellion, and a core of dedicated and able administrators kept England from actual bankruptcy and began to restore the state's defences against foreign invasion. They also restored the value of a debased currency, maintained, reformed and adapted the bureaucratic changes brought in by Wolsey and Cromwell and continued to direct an increasingly effective and legitimate network of courts, agents and judges across the land. There was plentiful disorder during the mid-Tudor period but law and administration continued to function.

The succession

More than anything else, it was Henry VIII's inability to produce a healthy male heir that blighted the latter half of his reign and, despite his best efforts and those of his best administrators, ensured that faction, usurpation and intrigue should dominate high politics from 1540 onwards. The lack of an ideal successor created the trauma of the royal divorce, the break with Rome, the rejection and judicial murder of Anne Boleyn, and the dizzying changes in wife and religion which marked the 1540s. It ensured the rule of the sickly boy and the fanatic Mary and placed a question mark over the future of Elizabeth, a royal figure, but still a woman.

The nightmare of early death and troubled regency which had wrecked the reigns of Henry VI and Edward V, and led to the shallow rule of both Edward IV and his brother Richard, came back to haunt the ageing Henry VIII.

Each royal courtship and marriage had offered opportunities to the competing conservatives and reformers of the Henrician court. The eclipse of Catherine of Aragon had done for Wolsey, that of Anne of Cleves had sunk Cromwell. The rise and fall of Catherine Howard saw the rise and fall of the Howards, and of Gardiner.

Behind each struggle lay the whole vexed question of religion. Each faction used adherence to one or other shade of opinion as a test of their progress and status. What the mid-Tudor period was to show was that the assumption that the great ones could simply decree religious opinion and that the lower sort would obligingly fall into line was increasingly flawed. When such religious loyalties among the great ones became mixed up with the succession there was little hope of stable rule.

Thus, the king's instrument of succession was subverted by Somerset for religious and factional reasons to wrong-foot the religious conservatives in 1547. Likewise, the duke of Northumberland tampered disastrously with the Tudor inheritance and paid the price. The strong appeal of legitimacy was indicated by the initial rallying of public opinion to the Catholic Queen Mary I. The need for a legitimate heir underpinned Mary's frantic desire for marriage, for pregnancy and eventually her acceptance of her sister's right to rule after her demise. It is possible to argue that this abiding willingness to accept the right to rule of each of Henry VIII's imperfect children indicates the essential underlying strength of the Tudor monarchy which survived where Yorkists and Lancastrians had struggled in the previous century. Nevertheless, such survival continued to entail constant struggle, faction, instability, foreign interference, and the threat of outright rebellion.

Faction

Faction was hardly unique to the middle years of the Tudor dynasty. It has been seen as pernicious by many historians, and deplored long into the nineteenth century by active politicians, but it has been reasonably argued that it was a necessary phenomenon for active and energetic government. However, in the absence of organised parties, the main requirement was that successful factions should stay successful long enough to provide stability, continuity and effectiveness. In the fifteenth century weak kingship and challenges to the succession had led to the rapid turnover of factions and rulers. The 'strong' rule of Henry VII and his son until 1540 had seen faction kept within bounds. Thus, when faction overthrew Wolsey from 1529 to 1530, its victory was shortlived. Thomas Cromwell's promotion from Wolsey's own household and his grasp of many of the essentials of the Cardinal's rule ensured stability. Once Cromwell was himself overthrown in 1540, an ailing, suspicious and in many ways inconsistent king seemed all too willing to allow conservative and radical or Catholic and Protestant factions to compete openly without allowing lasting victory for either.

As in the fifteenth century, uncertainty and a rapid turnover in the succession deprived factions of lasting victory. Thus, Somerset's party was succeeded by that of Northumberland. He was defeated by Mary's accession. Her promotion of the Catholic cause was, in turn, thwarted by her death. Under Elizabeth there remained all sorts of dangers, but despite the rise and fall of courtiers and officials, and the continued competing claims of great lords and comparative upstarts and of Catholic, Protestant and puritan hopes, faction returned to its role as an engine of politics. Moreover, the core of council and administration remained remarkably consistent at least until 1589. The great complicating factor which affected politics after 1533, and was particularly damaging in the years 1540 to 1563, was the identification of faction with differences of religion. Even then England, in marked contrast to her neighbours, was able to avoid the full rigours of outright civil war over religion.

Religion

The struggle between radicals and conservatives

As we have seen, religion had long been a complication in high and low politics since the twin challenges of Luther and Zwingli threatened the Catholic church in 1519. Henry VIII's assault upon the English church had been inseparable from his concern for the succession and his lust for Anne Boleyn. So, after her removal in 1536, Henry's quest for a wife and further heirs led to factional support for marital candidates combined with varying interpretations of the Henrician religious settlement. After Cromwell had combined a disastrous candidate (Anne of Cleves) with an excessive enthusiasm for a Lutheran twist to the settlement, the 1540s were characterised by a taut struggle between religious radicals and conservatives. In this the supposed triumph of the conservatives at Cromwell's fall was largely reversed by the unfortunate choice of the lascivious Catherine Howard as Henry's wife. The king's last years settled little and must have been somewhat confusing for genuinely enthusiastic believers. Throughout Henry's oscillations between executions of Protestant enthusiasts and unruly Catholic monks, between arraigning Cranmer for heresy and terrifying Queen Catherine

Parr on account of her Protestantism and crushing the Howard faction, a certain consistency emerges. For Henry was at least aware of the social implications of religious change and showed a firm sense of what he wanted. He did not want 'that precious jewel . . . the word of God rhymed and jangled in every alehouse'. He was dubious about clerical marriage, fairly sure of his adherence to the traditional sacraments and did not wish women or the lower classes to gain direct access to excessive knowledge of the Bible. The *King's book* and the 1547 *Book of homilies* show a sensible awareness of the use of worship to reinforce kingship and the social fabric. However, although the 'Exhortation concerning good order and obedience to rulers and magistrates' suggests a positive use of the pulpit, its subtext is a sense that religious change was subverting both good order and obedience.[1]

When Henry died in 1547, the official position of English religion may be summed up as the continued existence of an English Catholic church in which the sacraments were largely untouched, clerical marriage was not tolerated, the monastic orders had been swept away, the royal supremacy had superseded that of the pope and the old Mass was largely retained, but one in which service and Bible gave the worshipper access to the word of God in the vernacular.

However, this is to understate the position at court, where the dying king seems to have accepted the rise of the Protestant faction led by the Seymour brothers by banishing the conservative Gardiner from the council and imprisoning the duke of Norfolk. Furthermore, his appointment of Protestant tutors such as John Cheke to supervise his son's education was, whether intentionally or not, to be significant for the new reign, as was the survival of Cranmer.

Was there a crisis in religion?

It is difficult to argue against the concept of a mid-Tudor crisis in religion. Firstly, however, this was an era where the idea of *cuius regio eius religio* was well established in practice, at least in Germany. This was the principle that each state would accept the religion (*religio*) of the ruler of the region (*regio*) but this was hardly a source of stability, as the legitimate ruler of England changed in 1547, twice in 1553 and again in 1558.

Secondly, the rapid changes in the official line on religion in Henry's reign had meant that there was hardly a general awareness of, and confidence in, an agreed set of beliefs at all levels of society. This fact goes a long way towards explaining the general confused acquiescence of the bulk of the population. This was despite the very considerable and often violent regional resistance to the official policies adopted between 1547 and 1553 under Somerset and Northumberland. Likewise, although the subject of much dispute, it seems true that the rebellions against Mary were not primarily religious but arose for political and courtly reasons, as did Wyatt's Rebellion. They were a reaction against distress, as in the case of many of the disturbances in the last two years of her reign. Resistance to Mary's programme of re-Catholicisation was heroically displayed in the fires of Smithfield and in the martyrdoms of Bishops Latimer and Ridley and Archbishop Cranmer. However, the so-called Marian exiles prudently kept well away and, significantly, their exodus was accompanied by that of eminent figures in mid-Tudor society. Some of these came from court circles, and Mary made no attempt to halt or persecute them. Mary's victims were on the whole both stubborn and lower class, with the conspicuous exceptions of the bishops who were too prominent and, in Cranmer's case, too personally obnoxious to the queen, to be able to expect much mercy. In short, resistance to Mary's policy was confined to that minority of fully committed Protestants who were prepared to die for their beliefs. The possible leaders of a more determined pro-Protestant policy were prepared to sit things out. It is, of course, well worth considering whether such a policy would have been possible or desirable for potential Protestant leaders had Mary been younger or had borne children. The likelihood of a short reign and the succession of the more sympathetic Elizabeth probably counselled most Protestants to be patient.

Prospects for change

This brings us to the vexed question of whether either Edward VI's and Cranmer's option of radical Protestantism veering towards Zwinglianism or Mary's project of re-Catholicisation bore any real chance of success.

Clearly both projects were, in the short term, doomed due to the truncated lifespans of both rulers which denied them the chance to lay down the gradual grassroots measures that were ultimately to enable Elizabeth I to create a lasting national church.

Nevertheless, we know that the Cornish rebels rejected the first Edwardian Prayer Book with contumely as 'like unto a Christmas Game', while the appointment of continental radicals such as Peter Martyr to high rank (he was foisted upon Oxford University to considerable local outrage) indicates that English xenophobia was as sceptical of foreign radicals as it was of foreign Catholics. In the Edwardian Acts of Uniformity and even in Mary's own reliance upon parliament for her settlement we see that Henry and Cromwell's enthusiasm for issuing religious commands backed by statute confirmed a significant trend. Religious policy emerged from the central government where papal power had been replaced by the majesty of king *in parliament*. Even Mary's restoration of papal power relied on her to exercise her hated powers as head of the church before it could become the law of the land. Moreover, once religious uniformity became the law of the land it was up to Edward's government to enforce it against the Cornish, and for Mary to enforce it upon London and the south-east.

It is possible to suggest that both regimes were entirely capable of enforcing their separate projects. After all, both dealt successfully with the challenges of rebellion in 1549 and 1554 respectively. One is tempted to ascribe such hopes of success under Edward VI, as historian Nigel Heard does, to the fact that 'the whole of the period between 1547 and 1553 is held to be one of marked toleration'.[2] Edward's regime did not give waverers nor Catholics a particularly hard time and thus the uncommitted masses might well have acquiesced eventually. Likewise there is a traditional argument which suggests that 'the fruit of martyrs' witness' in Mary's reign was directly and profoundly counter-productive, where a subtler and more measured approach might have achieved lasting success.

Setting aside the fact that lasting success was not realistically achievable in the five years given to Mary, there is truth in this argument. We know that both Archbishop Gardiner and Philip II, neither of them notoriously soft-hearted, urged Mary to halt the killings. They were too well aware of the way the burnings were affecting public opinion.

An alternative might well have been to accept Cranmer's renunciation of the new Faith that he more than anyone other than the old king had done so much to create. It would have recovered with difficulty from such a body blow. In fact, Mary had had the sense to let the political and religious exiles out of the country, and to deal very uncontroversially with the fate of the church and monastic lands, much of which had passed irreversibly to the parliamentary classes. Even the Spanish alliance was an acceptably traditional arrangement for England, and had been going strong since the reign of Mary's grandfather. Perhaps all Mary really needed was time and a child.

There is even a half convincing argument that the Marian burnings were not entirely misguided. The extirpation of heresy by fire and sword, the deliberate gift of mass martyrdom to virtually whole populations was popular enough in parts of Germany, Poland, Spain and Italy. Thus, after the sixteenth-century wars of religion, there were probably none of the originally many Protestant converts left alive in Catholic Poland. Similarly, the numerous Protestant Utraquists of Bohemia, who wanted the laity to receive both the bread and wine at Mass, proved to be conspicuously thin on the ground after the Catholic victory in the Battle of the White Mountain during the Thirty Years War from 1618 to 1648. Similarly, *efficient* burnings such as Philip II's numerous *autos de fe* in Spain had proved remarkably effective in eliminating heresy. Under certain circumstances brutal extirpation evidently did work, although it can easily be argued that those circumstances were almost wholly absent in England from 1553 to 1558.

Conclusion

Was there, therefore, a crisis in religion between 1547 and 1563? Given the confusion, rebellion, plotting and faction that religious change engendered it is hard to deny that there was indeed a crisis. Following on from comment upon the Henrician break with Rome, it is quite clear that religious change struck at the heart of traditional or rather late-medieval concepts of authority, at high and low, central and local level.

Henry's assault on the pope, his humiliation of the clergy and his dissolution of the monasteries dismantled an entire edifice of traditional authority. The changing role of priests, monks and nuns, the changing definitions of the Mass and the attempt at Catholic restoration all confused and undermined previously accepted roles and authorities. Henry's own *King's book*, and the resort to homilies and adjurations, exemplify the official realisation that some dangerous and subversive genies were out of the bottle thanks to religious change. From the humblest parish priest to the burning of Cranmer, the highest priest in the land, we see one of society's long-standing props, clerical respect, called into question. It was left to Elizabeth to systematically try and put the pieces back together and to restore episcopacy and priesthood to a meaningful role as mainstays of the state.

Society and the economy

Riot, disorder and rebellion

As we have seen, there was a sense of turmoil and unease in the towns and countryside of Tudor England. However, the lawlessness arising from the Wars of the Roses, and the uncontrolled practice of Maintenance had been much restricted, while the powers of sheriffs and justices of the peace had been systematically restored and extended. In general, the king's peace had been restored.

Examination of riot, disorder and rebellion up to 1547, however, highlights the willingness of the commons to resist taxation and, in times of dearth, to resort to direct action. This ranged from food riots up to outright defiance such as that displayed in the Pilgrimage of Grace. Whatever the higher politics and religious sensibilities displayed in that rebellion, our analysis comes back to the hunger and depression of the commons in the North between 1536 and 1537. Increasingly the underlying crisis, later to be known as the Malthusian crisis[3] of overpopulation, unemployment, underemployment and insufficient and ill-distributed food resources, posed a recurrent danger to the king's peace. Starvation in the towns or the countryside could all too easily be translated into desperate violence and a challenge to the local or metropolitan regime. This was the reason for Wolsey's concern at the setting-up of enclosure commissions and his genuine interest in poor men's causes and for the threat posed to the Henrician project by the Pilgrimage of Grace.

Likewise, uncertainties and changes in high politics in the mid-Tudor period loosened the reins of central government so that dynastic trouble such as Wyatt's Rebellion, religious discontent as in the Cornish Rebellion or direct dispute over land and enclosure as in Kett's Rebellion could lead to a stark threat to the regime, backed by the recruitment of rebels who in hard times had little enough to lose.

In fact, poor harvests and the dreadful epidemics which characterised the mid-Tudor period probably took the edge off the Malthusian crisis. If a fifth of the population was lost during this period, then overpopulation would not became a problem until the hungry nineties.

A faltering economy

A remarkable series of unfortunate coincidences ensured that mid-Tudor governments faced a faltering economy. Besides the long-term problems of population growth and the need to grow, buy or distribute sufficient food for a larger population, there was a simple crisis of government revenue and spending. Thomas Cromwell had promised to make Henry VIII a uniquely rich king and, through the dissolution of the monasteries, was largely successful in doing so. However, Henry's ill-considered and extravagant foreign policy of the 1540s threw away the financial fruits of the break with Rome. Lengthy expeditions against France and Scotland suffered from the rapidly increasing growth in the cost of early modern warfare. Compared with Henry's early successes up to 1513, the new technologies and tactics of the 1540s were simply beyond the means of the late Henrician state. Henry's last wars were indulged in with appalling long-term consequences for the monarchy, but the ambitions of, successively, Somerset, Northumberland and even Mary (in her French war) compounded the problem. For mid-Tudor governments yielded to the fatal temptation to debase the currency. Before Henry's first debasement, coinage had contained an average 92.5 per cent silver. By 1551 the percentage had fallen to a mere 20 per cent. War, debasement and the inflation that stemmed from both wrecked the money supply and created a genuine financial crisis.[4]

Moreover, the cloth trade with the Spanish Netherlands via Antwerp collapsed at this time, through a combination of diplomatic and commercial constraints. The problem was exacerbated by the artificially high exports achieved by the debasement, and it played havoc with the English economy and the royal revenue.

Acts to manage poverty and vagrancy

The results of economic crisis can be seen in the statute book. Vagrancy Acts were introduced and amended in 1547 and 1549, while statutes for the relief of the poor appeared in 1552 and 1563. The full implications of the government's assumption of responsibility for the management of vagrancy and poverty deserves separate discussion. It suffices at this stage to note that central government was often led by local initiatives and that Tudor regimes at all levels displayed an interesting combination of coercion and paternalism which enable useful insights to be made into how authority saw itself and its responsibilities. In the 1540s and 1550s, it is clear that the weight of rebellion, food shortages, persistent vagrancy and economic depression combined to force the government into preventive and reactive legislation against all these ills.

The effects of religious change

Clearly there was an economic crisis in the mid-Tudor period which helps explain a great deal of the social and political unrest facing the regime. Now we must examine the social dimension.

It has already been suggested that religious change had undermined church authority. It is probably fair to suggest that both Edwardian Protestant enthusiasm and the Marian reaction must have disorientated many of the lower classes and inspired a degree of cynicism as foreign radicals and papist exiles alternated in handing down the prescriptions of successive Protestant and Catholic regimes.

Other interesting side effects of religious change were noted some time ago by social historians such as A. Macfarlane and Keith Thomas.[5] Their work suggested that the removal of the certainties of the Mass, confession, penance and Purgatory, and their replacement with often barely understood Protestant doctrines such as Justification by Faith Alone, and Predestination, caused significant changes in social and communal activities. It is likely that changes in the role of the parish priest, the new emphasis on Protestant individualism, the removal of monastic charity and the end of a belief in Purgatory profoundly affected understanding of the individual's role in rural society. Formerly, it was believed that the individual could shorten his or her time in Purgatory by charity and good works. The Protestant doctrine of Justification by Faith taught that salvation depended on faith alone. Beggars and vagrants were more numerous but traditional guidelines for their relief had been replaced by half-wrought, local and central government measures, while traditional death rituals must have been deeply disturbed by changes in doctrine. The results, argued Macfarlane and Thomas, seem to have been twofold. On the one hand, the development of the English witch-craze may have arisen partly from fear of the beggar's curse and the increasing lack of traditional ways of coping with the elderly and indigent now that Catholic forms of intercession and monastic alms-giving were gone. On the other, aspects of the old religion either went successfully underground (J. J. Scarisbrick argues strongly for Catholic resilience throughout the sixteenth century) or became absorbed and distorted into the body of traditional 'white' magic with Latin prayers returning as muttered spells. Such mutterings also, no doubt, overlapped into the popular perceptions surrounding the witch-craze.

Government intervention

In the context of a discussion of authority and disorder in general, and of the state of the crisis in mid-Tudor England in particular, it is possible to argue that a crisis of poverty and vagrancy was evident, that local and central government was stepping in, and that there was much confusion about levels of individual, communal, church and government responsibility for dealing with these evils. By the mid-sixteenth century, this confusion was being resolved by a variety of official and unofficial initiatives, ranging from the trial and execution of widow women for 'witchcraft' to the stockpiling of grain stores by individual city councils, and upwards to an evolving statute law on poverty and vagrancy.

Changes in land ownership

Other changes were also creating confusion and unrest at this time. The Henrician assault on church, monastery and chantry had released considerable wealth, especially in the form of land, into Tudor society. This process had been accelerated first by Henry's need to realise much of his loot in cash form. Thus, although the crown's lands were much extended, Henry could not afford to keep his wealth locked up in land.

He had expensive wars to pay for. There were obvious beneficiaries, not least among Thomas Cromwell's functionaries who had administered the dissolutions.

Richard Rich, Audley, Wriothesley all achieved both high office and considerable landed wealth. So too did the traditionally great. When Mary hankered after the restoration of church land, she was restrained not only by a parliament who owned much of that land but also by the knowledge that 'Catholic' supporters such as the duke of Norfolk also had deep vested interests in those estates.

Furthermore, new and long-standing landlords were engaged in activities such as enclosure and intensive sheep farming which were also having a major and often controversial impact on rural society. Cardinal Wolsey and the duke of Somerset both indicated government sensitivity towards the effects of such developments. Interestingly, both endured the furious criticism of the rest of the ruling class as such. There is evidence that the influence of John Hales and the so-called commonwealthmen upon Somerset, combined with his own incompetence and confusing policy signals, helped stir up a fair amount of the troubles associated with the rebellions of 1549.[6] New developments in commercial farming, together with enclosure and upheavals in the ownership of land across the country, seem to have come to a head after Henry's death. In both major rebellions, in the west and the east of the country, we find the role of the local elites under challenge. Kett was certainly in dispute over land and enclosure in East Anglia, sheep tax and food prices were among the early complaints of the Cornish rebels, while the elite seem to have been divided over religious sympathies.

It is also interesting to examine the ambivalence of a senior figure such as Sir Peter Carew, who was outstandingly on the side of the regime in helping suppress the 1549 rising in the west, and yet was himself a rebel against Mary in 1554. He seemed unable to command significant support in the west during his own revolt, presumably because of his role in suppressing the commons five years earlier.[7]

Document case study
Agrarian problems

5.1 Rebellion in Norfolk

Kett's demands being in rebellion, 1549

1. We pray your grace that where it is enacted for enclosing that it be not hurtful to such as have enclosed saffren [a plant used in the manufacture of worsted cloth] grounds for they be greatly chargeable to them, and that from henceforth no man shall enclose anymore.

2. We pray your grace that no lord of no manor shall come on upon the Commons.

Source: A. Fletcher, *Tudor rebellions*, London, 1983, pp. 120–21

5.2 Problems caused by enclosures

From A discourse of the commonweal of this realm of England, *written by Sir Thomas Smith around 1549*

Husbandman: Marry for these enclosures do undo us all, for they make us pay dearer for our land that we occupy . . . all is taken for pastures, either for sheep or grazing of cattle. By these enclosures men do lack livings and be idle . . . Moreover, all things are so dear that by their daily labour they are not able to live.

Capper: I have well experience thereof, for I am fain to give my journeymen 2d a day more than I was wont to do, and yet they say they cannot sufficiently live thereon. And by reason of such dearth as ye speak of, we that are artificers can keep few or no apprentices like as we were wont to do.

Source: Denys Cook, *The sixteenth century, documents and debates*, Basingstoke, 1980, pp. 63–64

5.3 Enclosure and engrossing

The modern historian, A. L. Beier, comments on the problems

Another mobile group were small-holders, who were forced out of, if not evicted from, common-field villages undergoing agrarian changes. These were usually described as 'enclosures', but the process was more complicated than just erecting fences . . . [it] involved the change to individual farming from a communal system in open fields. The result was the extinction of common rights . . .

Engrossing . . . was another menace to the small man. It involved the absorption of entire farms into larger units, usually for sheep farming.

Source: A. L. Beier, *The problem of the poor in Tudor and Stuart England*, London, 1983, p. 9

5.4 The increase in country rogues

Edward Hext, a Somerset justice of the peace, writes in a letter to Lord Burghley, 1596

I do not see how it is possible for the poor countryman to bear the burthens duly laid upon him . . . [they say] that the rich men have gotten all into their hands and will starve the poor. And I must justly say that the infinite numbers of the Idle wandering people and robbers of the land are the chiefest cause of the dearth . . . the most dangerous are the wandering soldiers and other stout rogues of England.

Source: John Pound, *Poverty and vagrancy in Tudor England*, London, 1971, pp. 94–95

Document case-study questions

1 In 5.1 and 5.2, why are the country folk so anxious about the commons? Who gained and who lost during the process of enclosure?

2 From 5.2, 5.3 and 5.4, how far do you think enclosure and engrossing created problems of both poverty and law and order?

3 Compare 5.1 to 5.4 with 4.1 to 4.4. What may have been the consequences for traditional deference towards landowners as a result of these agrarian concerns? How far had gentlemen damaged the order spoken of in 4.4 by enclosure and engrossing?

Notes and references

1 See G. R. Elton, *The Tudor constitution: documents and commentary*, Cambridge, 2nd edn, 1982, p. 15.

2 Nigel Heard, *Edward VI and Mary: a mid-Tudor crisis?*, London, 1990, p. 66.

3 So called after the Reverend Malthus who, writing in 1798 at the time of the Industrial Revolution, argued that rises in population always outstripped improvements in food production and that therefore the human race was subject to crises such as famine, war and pestilence in order to curb excess population.

4 This is well dealt with in S. J. Gunn, *Early Tudor government, 1485–1558*, London, 1995, pp. 129–31.

5 Alan Macfarlane and Keith Thomas, *Witchcraft in Tudor and Stuart England*, London, 1970. See the Select bibliography for more recent changes in theory.

6 G. R. Elton, *Reform and Reformation*, London, 1977, pp. 343–46 deals very well with the effects of Hales's advice.

7 A. Fletcher, *Tudor rebellions*, London, 1968, pp. 43–46, and 69–71.

6 The Celtic nations

In dealing with authority and disorder, some consideration of the other nations within the British Isles is inescapable. This is not least because the Tudor regimes drastically changed the nature of the relationship between England and her neighbours, Wales, Scotland and Ireland.

The most conspicuous and formal change came with the Union of England and Wales in 1536. Wales had been thoroughly and lastingly pacified long before, yet had, in recent years, formed the springboard for the Tudors' own usurpation of the crown. The quasi-independence of the Marcher lords, the maintenance of a Council in the Marches of Wales, the sporadic lawlessness of the border counties posed problems for the early Tudors not unlike the similar difficulties in maintaining quiet, good order and loyalty among the barons of the north country. Union resolved these problems to a degree, and it is significant that Wales provided no major resistance to the Reformation, and no support for the kind of rebellions that bedevilled the west, east and north of England. Wales was quiet, where many areas of the English periphery emphatically were not.

Wales

The Union

Thomas Cromwell seems to have marked out the better government of Wales as a project from about 1532. As such, the Act of Union and associated legislation complements the much greater process of administrative reform associated with Cromwell. This is borne out by the fact that key legislation was produced by the last session of the Reformation Parliament in 1536. The thinking behind Union was undoubtedly underpinned by English worries about possible foreign invasion.

Norman lords

In many ways Wales posed straightforward problems. The ancient division between the Marches and the Principality constantly led to smuggling and the flight of wanted criminals across the borders. Meanwhile the Marcher lords, notably Edward Stafford, the duke of Buckingham and the earl of Worcester, possessed a dangerous independence. Buckingham's ambitions and position had led famously to his judicial murder in 1521. Part of Cromwell's project was simply to end the lords' independence. Marches and Principality were duly merged in 1536 and the old Norman lordships were abolished.

Rowland Lee

Another straightforward challenge was the level of crime. Under a newly re-established Council in the Marches of Wales, Cromwell appointed Rowland Lee, bishop of Coventry and Lichfield, as Lord President in 1534. This formidable figure is said to have hanged no less than 5,000 criminals in nine years. This aspect of pacification was undertaken with notorious relish, while a programme of rebuilding and renovation of the border castles improved general security.

Although Lee seems to have been deficient in tact and subtlety the crown was prepared to go to any lengths to minimise the possibility of disturbances. In general, it was lucky that no major figure survived among the traditional Welsh aristocracy to act as a focus for opposition. The potentially dangerous Rhys Ap Griffiths, who might have rallied Catholic opinion, was dead and the majority of the Welsh 'gentry' seemed content to accept the abolition of all Welsh land law and the extension of English law and administrative structures throughout Wales peaceably. Indeed, the period from 1536 to 1640 has been known as 'the age of the gentry' in Wales. The new religious proposals under the Henrician Reformation were accepted, as in the past, without protest.

The new religion

There was a fair amount of occasional conformity among the Welsh during the Henrician and Edwardian Reformations and they seem to have remained quiescent and relatively untroubled by the Marian reaction. There were only three Welsh martyrs, although this may have had more to do with geography and the priorities of Mary's government. The Reformation was much sweetened by the availability of church lands. The key beneficiaries of the new order seem to have been the high-born freemen, described by J. Gwynfor Jones, the historian of early modern Wales, as 'a virile if economically restricted class of landed proprietors who enjoyed regional domination'.[1] In short, a bargain had been struck between the Tudor regime and these 'vested interests (which) ensured that the majority increasingly attached themselves to the tenets of the new Faith'. The freemen occupied themselves as the administrators of the new order, and in the congenial task of building up their family estates and connections. Represented after 1536 in the Westminster parliament, the Welsh were involved in the detail of the post-Cromwellian legislation of 1543, survived Mary and accepted the Elizabethan settlement without demur. By then the first Welsh book had been printed in 1546 and Elizabeth's regime required that Welsh and English Bibles be available in all the region's churches.

Order and disorder

Gwynfor Jones states that 'family and kindred feuds were as severe in Wales after the Act of Union as they had been before' and contemporary administrators complained about the tug of loyalties between kin and the state. In contrast to the position in Ireland and Scotland, however, the clans were vastly diminished in importance, the old religion was of little potency and the continued tradition of feuds, mayhem and payment of blood-money within Wales seems, as we shall see, to have been on no greater a scale than in many parts of England itself. In the maintenance of a distinctive Tudor order and in the keeping of the king's peace, policy in Wales was a distinct success.

Ireland

The origin of the Irish question

Ireland posed obvious problems in terms of the security of the realm and the Tudors used characteristic means to resolve them with, it is probably fair to say, appalling results.

As in Wales, a principal source of unease for the Tudors was to be found in the conduct of the long established Norman lordships. Although dating back to the reign of Henry II, English rule in Ireland was far more precarious than in Wales. The Norman lords had long since 'gone native' and could not merely be abolished. The Tudor state had to work in partnership with key members of this Anglo-Irish nobility and had to manipulate the incessant feuding and clan rivalries of the Irish, where possible, to advantage. The early years of Henry VII's reign had seen real danger threaten from Ireland, which provided succour to both Simnel and Warbeck and which forced Henry, through the new Lord Deputy, Edward Poynings, to extend English involvement. Crucially, Ireland during these years was seen as a convenient stick with which ambitious foreign rivals, notably the French, could beat the English.

Firstly, Simnel gained the recognition of the earl of Kildare, head of the Geraldine family, in 1486 and was only defeated with some difficulty at the Battle of Stoke. Then, in 1495, Perkin Warbeck appeared, gaining the support of another key Anglo-Norman, the earl of Desmond. Although Warbeck's forces were frustrated at the siege of Waterford and he was forced to try again from Scotland, it seemed that the Norman lords were wholly untrustworthy. Poynings remained in Ireland, and the Irish parliament was subordinated to the English under Poynings' Law, whereby no bill could be introduced into the Irish parliament without the consent of the king. Kildare was brought to England and, for a short time, imprisoned. However, Henry seems to have balked at the potential expense of direct rule at this time and chose to reinstate Kildare to maintain English authority beyond the Pale.

The revolt of Silken Thomas

Henry VIII was content to maintain his father's policy until the revolt of Silken Thomas. This was provoked initially by Thomas Cromwell's policy change in detaining Garret og Fitzgerald, the ninth earl of Kildare, in England in 1534, replacing him as Governor with an Englishman, Sir William Skeffington. Kildare's son, Thomas Fitzgerald, Lord Offaly, reacted by proclaiming a Catholic crusade against the heretical king and his kinsmen in 1534. As this occurred in the middle of the Henrician Reformation and at a time of considerable sensitivity over national security, it was felt that the Geraldines had become intolerable. A large army was despatched and the rebellion crushed. Thomas and five uncles were subjected to exemplary execution. The subsequent appointment of the soldier, Sir Edward Grey, to rule as Lord Deputy was a disaster. The Anglo-Irish lords resented his aggression outside the Pale and formed a League that assaulted the colony and went so far as to offer the sovereignty of Ireland to the king of Scotland in 1540. Henry was driven, therefore, to assert his kingship rather than lordship over Ireland in what has been described as a constitutional revolution. In theory, by so doing, Henry would be bound to extend good government over the whole island while the vexed question of land ownership would be resolved by a process known as 'surrender and regrant'. By this process the Anglo-Irish confirmed their land tenure under the king after first surrendering their lands to him. It involved the rejection of the pope's authority, the assumption of an English title and the adoption of the English language and modes of dress. With the surrender of key players such as the earl of Desmond and Con O'Neill, who became the first earl of Tyrone, this policy seemed to have hopes of success. However, it was abruptly suspended in 1543 when Henry embarked upon his French and Scottish Wars. This suspension, it is argued by Brendan Bradshaw,[2] was a key tragedy, leaving Ireland to the haphazard measures that followed.

Plantation policy

For good reasons mid-Tudor regimes, including Henry's after 1543, were not primarily concerned with Ireland. Both Edward VI and Mary I encouraged plantation policy. This was a kind of private enterprise colonialism which combined with religious enthusiasms to wreak havoc upon the native Irish and lastingly embitter Anglo-Irish relations. Under Edward, the duke of Somerset hit upon the use of settlers of proven loyalty to consolidate confiscated lands. These had been made vacant in the suppression of some of the leading Anglo-Irish and Irish families in the regions of Leix and Offaly, subsequently renamed Queen's and King's Counties. In 1556, Mary appointed Sir Thomas Ratcliffe (later earl of Sussex and a considerable grandee under Elizabeth) to direct plantations based upon the English manorial system. Although these plantations brought significant improvements in law and order and were administered with some efficiency, they inevitably provoked violence and resistance from the resentful and dispossessed natives. Moreover, Sussex was deeply unpopular with the inhabitants of the Pale itself. He promoted Englishmen to key offices within the government, raised and used large armies and inflicted high taxes and requisitions upon the Palesmen. He was ousted in 1564.

The religious issue

Ironically Mary was somewhat restrained in her religious policy towards Ireland. This was partly because of the obvious fact that Ireland was barely attached to the new religion anyway. More ominously, in the long term, it seems that Mary recognised the danger of too openly encouraging the religious opinions of the bulk of the Irish population at the expense of an exposed English ruling minority.

The Irish were always unlikely to accept the Protestant settlement imposed by Elizabeth with the equanimity shown by the Welsh. Moreover, that settlement was to be accompanied, after the fall of Sussex, by a comprehensive attempt by the English to conquer the whole of Ireland outside the Pale. Already Sean O'Neill, the new earl of Tyrone, was in defiance of the regime and was advocating resistance specifically as a Catholic leader against English heresy. Although he was murdered by the Macdonalds of Antrim, he had set a pattern that would be taken up by others.

The Enterprise of England

Between 1565 and 1578, apart from a brief respite under the less ambitious direction of Sir William Fitzwilliam, Sir Henry Sidney, as Lord Deputy of Ireland, extended plantation policy and conquest to degrees of brutality and treachery that, entirely predictably, threw all Ireland into violent disarray.

Attempts to break up existing large estates and to colonise much of Ulster were accompanied by the use of ruthless and irresponsible adventurers, such as Sir Peter Carew and Robert Devereux, earl of Essex, to set up their own plantation schemes. Murder bordering on genocide resulted as the native Irish and existing landholders were driven from their land and Protestant enclaves were established, often with only very temporary success. These schemes were part of the wider Enterprise of England, which saw adventurers and freebooters seeking land, trade and sometimes religious liberty across the known world. Puritans, frustrated by Elizabeth's policies at home, sought refuge in Ireland and North America. They treated the native Irish much as they treated the native American. Small wonder that the Irish resisted desperately. By 1578 the Palesmen, together with the earls of Ormond and Kildare, indicated to Elizabeth that Sidney's uninhibited policies were likely to provoke an all-Ireland revolt. Sidney was removed. However, it was too late, for Ireland had attracted the attention of other forces engaged in the wider European struggle.

The reconversion of the Irish

When James Fitzmaurice Fitzgerald landed in Ireland in July 1579 and pronounced a rebellion which was taken up by the earl of Desmond, he was accompanied by soldiers financed by Pope Gregory XIII and by Jesuit missionaries. Indeed from 1577 onwards Ireland was subject, but with striking success, to the same sort of missions of seminarists and Jesuits which were reaching the mainland. The Protestant Reformation had never convincingly impinged upon the native Irish, while clumsy and bloody English policies of government firmly identified Protestantism as the religion of the oppressor.

Revolt became more or less endemic. The Desmond rising was crushed and his estates deliberately subjected to a murderous famine. Within the Pale, during 1580, the new Lord Deputy, Arthur, Lord Grey, busied himself executing prominent members of the gentry, thus alienating the Palesmen further. When Desmond and his fellows were attainted, the Anglo-Irish lords rallied in opposition. By 1590, the three southern counties of Ireland were under military occupation and the English were again encroaching upon the O'Neill estates of the earl of Tyrone in Ulster. Reluctantly, the Great O'Neill was driven into revolt in

The Irish chiefs and their leader, O'Neill, submitting to the English Lord Deputy after their defeat in 1603. Tudor policy towards Ireland mirrored plantation policy in the New World and became disastrously entangled with religious conflict. Arguably, Irish policy was the least successful of Tudor efforts to govern the Celtic peoples of Britain.

1595 and, by 1596, had successfully appealed across all Ireland for support. The war would last till 1603, attract Spanish invasion, cost possibly millions of pounds and countless lives and lastingly poison the joint histories of England and Ireland. Tudor policy in Ireland was not a success.

Scotland

Where Ireland posed problems of conquest and submission, relations with Scotland were often characterised by opportunity. The Tudors were constantly threatened and seduced by the involvement of Scotland with the Tudor succession. The 'Auld Alliance', between France and Scotland, was, of course, an important factor in Anglo-Scottish relationships throughout the period.

Flowers of the field

Henry VII suffered from the ambitions not only of the pretender, Perkin Warbeck, who, in 1495, attracted a welcome, royal endorsement, a high-born marriage (the king's cousin) and military help on his arrival at the court of James IV. The invasion of 1496 fizzled out when there was no matching English revolt, as Warbeck had promised. However, Henry VII was convinced of the need to keep Scottish ambition at bay, concluding a truce in 1497 and a lasting peace and marriage alliance in 1503. This marriage between James IV and Henry VIII's sister Margaret was to prove lastingly awkward, begetting as it did the most trouble-some of all claimants to the Tudor succession in the form of Mary Queen of Scots.

This peace with James IV could not last. The Scottish king was eager to test the limits of English patience and found that the young King Henry VIII was only too anxious to embark upon warfare, primarily in re-opening the old quarrel with France, with which Henry remained fixated throughout his life. Inevitably Scotland was drawn into this war by the 'Auld Alliance'.

Not for the last time that century the Scots played into English hands. The Battle of Flodden, in 1513, was a catastrophe in which the flower of the Scottish aristocracy, the king and the king's son and heir perished. The event is still bathetically celebrated in one of Scotland's several unofficial national anthems.

England's opportunity

For years, Scotland ceased to be a threat to England. Henry VIII's sister ruled the country steadily with a series of regents. There was of course the ever-present danger on the borders where raiding and mayhem remained commonplace, as in much of the remoter provinces of the Tudor realm.

Trouble returned in the 1540s when war between England and France once more threatened. A further factor had by then intruded. The advent of the Henrician Reformation meant that war against Scotland might in certain circumstances become a religious crusade.

Once more the conflict took on an element of farce, when an invading Scottish army of 10,000 men was routed by 3,000 Englishmen at Solway Moss in 1542. James V died on receiving the news, either from shame or apoplexy, leaving as heir the infant Mary Queen of Scots. Briefly the prospect of a marriage between Mary and the future Edward VI beckoned. This would have united Tudor and Stuart and have had major implications for the relations between Scotland, England and France. It was not to be.

The rough wooing

An attempted agreement upon these lines in the Treaty of Greenwich was rejected by the Scots, with its government falling increasingly into the hands of the French party. When the future duke of Somerset launched an invasion in 1544, known ironically as the 'rough wooing', he took Protestant Bibles with him and behaved with a counter-productive brutality which left Scots embittered and inclining to the French for the next quarter of a century. As in Ireland, Tudor policy seemed to incline towards a careless brutality, which combined with an uncertainty of aims and ambitions to produce lasting instability.[3]

A Scottish Reformation

War continued under Somerset and his successor, Northumberland, until 1552, when the border was re-fixed where it had been before Henry VIII's futile campaigns. By then, the French were in charge, but many Scottish nobles, and the Lowlanders who had accepted the Protestant Faith, were naturally suspicious of the French and had no more wish to be a French than an English satellite. In fact, the French overplayed their hand. The regent, Mary of Guise, was given to appointing French co-religionists and seemed to be about to attempt the suppression of Protestantism. This provoked the Scottish Protestants into a successful revolt in which the Presbyterian influence of John Knox brought inspiration and coherence.

The chance succession of Mary Queen of Scots' husband, Francis, to the throne of France and the overweening ambition of the Guises led to plans not only for a large French invasion force but for the assertion of Mary's claim to the English throne. Elizabeth was persuaded reluctantly to commit troops to Scotland, the weather scattered the invasion fleet, and Scotland was safe, apparently, for Protestantism.

A scandalous queen

The sudden death of Francis II brought Mary's unexpected return from France. Elizabeth and her ministers, in trying to manipulate her away from French intrigue, probably overreached themselves, particularly in the totally unsuitable marriage set up for her with Lord Darnley. In fact, in Anglo-Scottish terms, Mary's brief reign turned out very well for Elizabeth. This was due to Mary's apparent attractiveness to the opposite sex, which was clearly still working far into the 1580s, and to her almost total lack of judgement or discretion. Admittedly, conduct of public affairs among the brutal and hardbitten Scottish Lords of the Covenant would have unnerved the most experienced of stateswomen, and did for the next two English surrogates Moray and Lennox. Nevertheless, in the circumstances of a newly established puritan Reformation, her apparent involvement in the murder of her second husband and her undoubted adultery with Bothwell were intolerable, and she was evicted from her throne with popular support.

James and the succession

Mary caused a great deal of unnecessary heartache south of the border during her long captivity. Yet subject to the incessant quarrels and faction of the Scottish court, the regency of the infant James worked out well, as did his own long kingship before he succeeded Elizabeth in England. In practice, the Wars of Religion left the French too preoccupied to stir up much mischief in Scotland. Moreover, from the early 1570s onwards, the French were increasingly inclined towards alliances, even marriage alliances, and towards co-operation with England. Although Philip II was happy to encourage Mary's plotting and ultimately took up her claim to the English throne, he had no hold over the Scots.

As he grew older, James showed discretion regarding his likely succession to Elizabeth. He grew adept, too, at manipulating the Scottish notables and was able to restore working episcopacy to the Scottish Church. After 1559, Tudor policy in Scotland must be seen as a success, although arguably Elizabeth's refusal to condemn Mary outright, or to execute her when evidence of her treachery had become commonplace, prolonged difficulties far longer than was necessary.

Order and disorder

The Scottish borders remained turbulent, as did Scottish politics, while the highland clans remained Catholic and steeped in a culture based upon warfare and vendetta. Scotland, too, was the scene of a long-lasting and probably more intense witch-craze than England. However, the strict moral code of a Calvinist Reformation and the disciplines the new Faith brought to household and parish greatly advanced the civilisation of the Lowlands, safe from the depredations of English invasion. Conversely, the ultimate success of Tudor policy towards Scotland preserved national security on England's northern border till the Bishops' Wars of 1639–40, an achievement comparable to that in Wales.

The consequences of Tudor policy

In maintaining authority against disorder and the threat of war, the Tudors would always have been forced to concentrate on the Celtic periphery. Wales, Scotland and Ireland had all provided bases for foreign invasion and usurpation of the crown, and Scotland and Ireland would do so again. The task in Wales was the simplest of the three. A long-conquered nation, it needed to be consolidated and assimilated into England's laws and administration. This, with comparatively little disturbance, was achieved. The shires and counties of England were replicated in Wales and the justices of the peace, co-opted from among the gentry, administered the laws. Now Welsh representatives debated at Westminster, and the Established Church of England was established, too, in Wales.

In Scotland there were brief opportunities for a similar degree of political union which were lost, partly through the resolute clumsiness of English policy in the 1540s. In the absence of that union, the English benefited less than they might have done from any brilliance or subtlety in policy. Instead, England gained more from the achievements of the Scottish Presbyterians and the Lords of the Covenant, from the overambition and incompetence of the French, and from the foolishness of Mary. Scotland retained her own laws and religious establishment, and her own king and, like England and Wales, shared in the benefits of a better educated, literate, even peaceful era.

In Ireland, however, religious and civil strife, racial murder and oppression characterised the sixteenth century. The native Irish were starved and driven off their land, feuding and clan warfare persisted and authority, where it existed at all, in or out of the Pale, was enforced by lethal violence. Disorder thrived in Ireland.

Notes and references

1 The key text on Wales is J. Gwynfor Jones, *Early modern Wales, 1525–1640*, Basingstoke, 1994. S. Gunn, *Early Tudor government*, Basingstoke, 1995, pp. 62–70 is useful on both Ireland and Wales. See also T. Herbert and G. Elwys Jones, *Tudor Wales*, Milton Keynes, 1988.

2 Brendan Bradshaw, *The Irish constitutional revolution in the sixteenth century*, Cambridge, 1979; see also Henry Jeffries, 'The Frontier Regions', in J. Lotherington (ed.), *The Tudor years*, London, 1994, pp. 334–75.

3 G. R. Elton, *Reform and Reformation*, London, 1977, pp. 340–42 covers the 'rough wooing' carried out by Somerset's army. Lotherington, *Tudor years*, pp. 303–8 deals well with Mary Queen of Scots.

7 Elizabeth I and the recovery of monarchy

The position in 1558

When Elizabeth I inherited the throne from her unfortunate and little lamented sister, she possessed several distinct advantages over her predecessor. Firstly, there was the triumph of hope which had once helped Mary herself. A new reign always created fresh expectations and, in politics and religion in particular, posed attractive new opportunities for those excluded from the benefits of the previous reign. Her equivocal position regarding religion, at least at first, created sympathies from all sides. She was Anne Boleyn's daughter and therefore a focus for Protestant hopes. Yet she was not known for her fierce commitment but more for her appreciation of the ceremonies, vestments, incense and candles of traditional religious observance. Most of all, like Mary, she benefited from powerful prejudice in favour of the Tudor dynasty. She, too, was the daughter of the great King Henry.

In fact she inherited the throne when, for a brief period of time, the very worst of a series of apparent crises seemed over. Harvests were picking up, Sir Thomas Gresham, the merchant and financier, was well on the way to restoring the coinage and the worst of trade slumps had passed. Not unconnected to these positive developments was the return of a general peace. Not only were England's specific and ruinous conflicts at an end but so, too, for the time being, were the religious wars in Germany (the Peace of Augsburg had been signed between Charles V and the Protestant princes in 1555). Moreover, with the signing of the Treaty of Cateau-Cambrésis in 1559, the conflict between Habsburg and Valois had ended. Indeed, for the first ten years of her reign the centrepiece of Tudor foreign policy, the Spanish alliance, remained in place. Crucially, Philip II was anxious at first to reassure the new queen of his friendship and even to offer himself in marriage.

Peace brought a rise in trade and, therefore, an improvement in government finances, while removing the horrendous drain posed by Somerset's, Northumberland's and Mary's wars (quite apart from Henry VIII's excesses).

One of the queen's great virtues, at least at first, was her abhorrence of the expense of war which, combined with her increasingly legendary inability to make up her mind on foreign policy issues, kept England out of major European conflict until 1585. Realistically or not, she always considered that vigorous foreign policy adventures should be profitable. The small wars of Hawkins and Drake were run as private enterprises with profits ideally accruing to the crown.

Administration under Elizabeth

Continuity

Like her father before her, Elizabeth was forced to retain a number of her predecessor's councillors. Where Henry VIII had removed and executed the unpopular Empson and Dudley, but had retained the services of long-established administrators such as Fox and Warham, so Elizabeth was swift to remove obstinate Marians such as Heath and Cheney. The retention and promotion of William Cecil (later Lord Burghley) was a recognition both of genuine experience and ability and of past and future loyalty. Below the level of privy council, continuity was the watchword with figures such as Thomas Gresham maintaining their successful administration from earlier reigns.

Significantly, however, Elizabeth packed her council with relatives derived from the Boleyn and Howard families. This was almost certainly a hangover from the insecurities she had suffered in the dangerous courts of Henry, Edward and Mary. Indeed, later in her reign, it was notable that the next generation of councillors were frequently the sons and heirs of her first council.[1]

Cromwell's legacy

Historians such as Penry Williams and others have long since disproved the more grandiose claims made by G. R. Elton regarding Thomas Cromwell's so-called 'revolution in government'. The reformed privy council of Cromwell's day had been superseded by Mary's larger, more traditional and unwieldy body. In addition, the famous revenue courts, established to handle the riches of the dissolutions and the plundering of the old church, had become redundant as those riches were squandered in the expensive wars of the mid-Tudor period.[2] However, the administrators of the new regime were bureaucrats, direct heirs of Cromwell's men of business. Rich, Audley and Wriothesley had been succeeded by Petre, Paulet and Cecil. Strikingly, the office of Principal Secretary which had formed Cromwell's power base remained of critical importance in the Elizabethan regime, in the safe hands of William Cecil, Francis Walsingham and later, Robert Cecil. It was also significant that, whatever the riches and offices acquired by many of Elizabeth's most glamorous protégés such as Walter Ralegh and the earl of Essex, they were increasingly kept well away from the inner ring of the council. Although there were important overlaps, notably in the persons of Burghley and Leicester, there was a distinct difference in function and status between council and court.

Statute and parliament

A notable survivor of Cromwell's 'system' was the maintenance of supremacy of statute and with it the growing power and prestige of parliament. Cromwell enormously increased Henry VIII's power as 'king in parliament' but, in doing so, he had involved parliament in the debate and passage of each aspect of the Reformation process. Matters of religious settlement, the future of the succession and the disposition of vast resources of wealth and land had been subject to parliamentary legislation. Moreover, the lengthy sessions of the Reformation Parliament and its successors had increased the coherence, political sophistication and status of members of the Commons and Lords. After Henry's death, the religious, political, economic and social policies of Seymour and Dudley had been subject to the same supremacy of statute. Ironically much of Mary's project to reimpose Catholicism was subject to the same fate, not least when she reversed much Reformation legislation using her powers under the royal supremacy. Likewise, any hope of restoring church land to the old Catholic establishment was frustrated by the awkward fact that the greatest redistribution of that very land had been to the members of the Commons and Lords who were not going to vote to reverse their own gains.

The religious settlement

The queen was genuinely Protestant. However, for at least the first half of her reign, she not only worked hard to avoid giving unnecessary offence to Catholics, but deeply frustrated her Protestant subjects by adopting a stubborn and conservative approach to the most overt areas of doctrine and church policy, such as the wearing of vestments and the importance given to preaching. Like her father she was distrustful of a preaching clergy and of over-widespread access to the unvarnished words of the Scriptures. Furthermore, she ignored the most reform-minded of the Marian exiles and forced their Protestant colleagues to implement distasteful policies that were in many ways the reverse of their own aspirations. Able and sincere Protestants such as Jewel, Cox and even Grindal had to enforce and defend Archbishop Parker's 1566 Advertisements which enforced the wearing of vestments. They also had to suppress Bible readings and prophesyings – meetings of local clergy to hear one another preach.

In fact, there were good reasons of state behind much of Elizabeth's policy. She was able to appease Philip II and retain the Spanish alliance for most of her first decade of rule and, most importantly, she aimed with some success to let native Catholicism wither on the vine. Tepidly persecuted by inconsistently enforced recusancy laws, most native Catholics remained loyal enough, although Elizabeth paid the price in the understandable fury and frustration of ardent Protestant subjects who wished her to become their Deborah or Queen Gloriana.[3] She would not, however, cast herself in the role of leader of Protestant Europe despite the constant and often downright irritating pleas of figures as disparate as her favourite Leicester, her spy-master Walsingham, the importunate preacher Stubbs, the parliament men, Paul and Peter Wentworth, and the downright offensive Marprelate writers. These aims lasted for most of the reign, from the importunate demands that the queen marry and name a successor in the parliament of 1562, to the crude protests against her wooing of the duke of Anjou between 1578 and 1580, through to the imprisonment of the outspoken Peter Wentworth as late as 1593.

Foreign fears

The threat of invasion

The danger of foreign invasion was to dominate the latter half of Elizabeth's reign, with the Great Armada of 1588 succeeded by a number of Ireland-bound armadas, one of which did manage to land troops and link with Irish rebels. This worry had not affected her predecessors since the early years of Henry VII's reign. Then Henry had had good reason to worry. His challenges to Richard III, and those of earlier Lancastrians against the House of York, had been launched from France and Burgundy. Likewise, Henry had to contend with two pretenders, Simnel and Warbeck, who drew substantial support from France, Scotland and Ireland.

After Charles VIII of France's descent upon Italy in 1494, such danger was greatly lessened as the Italian wars then merged into a lengthy period of Habsburg–Valois rivalry. England's role was further limited by the rising costs of modern warfare until the ill-judged interventions of Henry VIII in the 1540s. These conclusively proved that England simply lacked the economic clout to be a major player in the European rivalries of the period.

Yet danger threatened briefly during the lull in Habsburg–Valois conflict in the mid-1530s. This was enough to frighten Henry and later helped to defeat Cromwell's pro-Protestant alignment based on the marriage between Henry and Anne of Cleves.

The Spanish alliance

The alliance with Spain, originating with the match between Catherine of Aragon and Henry VIII's brother, Arthur (and since severely tested by the divorce), had been more or less a constant throughout the century. This was bolstered, of course, by the traditional hatred of the French. Indeed, revivals of the alliance in the 1540s and 1550s had been based upon traditional hankerings after the ports of Calais and Boulogne, the last relics of England's triumphs in the Hundred Years War.

Diplomatic revolution

English xenophobia had reared its head in the riots against foreigners of the 'Evil May Day' of 1517, and again in the grievances of the supporters of the Wyatt Rebellion of 1554. The latter resented the alleged influence of the Spanish beneficiaries of Mary's marriage to Philip II. However, Mary's marriage had undoubtedly occurred at the expense of possibly disgruntled English candidates. The alliance with Spain against France was not unnatural for it fitted into a tradition dating back to Catherine of Aragon's marriage to Arthur, but both events derived unpopularity from the expense involved, and from the lack of military success in general and from the loss of Calais in particular.

When Elizabeth came to the throne, Philip offered his hand in marriage. Over the first decade of her rule, it seems to have been the expectation of the pope and Philip that Elizabeth would somehow, and soon, return the realm to the true

Faith. By the late 1560s, as the dust settled on Elizabeth's settlement and the recusancy laws bit (no matter how gently), it was clear that this was not going to happen. Successive Spanish ambassadors were revealed in treasonous plotting with Englishmen against the queen, and the Revolt of the Northern Earls of 1569, followed by the papal bull of *Regnans in Excelsis,* further soured relations between Elizabeth and her former ally. Other and earthier matters contributed, notably Hawkins's first slaving voyages to the New World from 1565 onwards, and the scandalous provocation afforded when Elizabeth impounded the duke of Alva's treasure in 1568.

The Black Legend

Elizabeth's sailors provoked the Spanish, who particularly detested the pirate, Francis Drake. English sailors and travellers accordingly suffered torture and burning if captured, not least under the anti-heretic laws of Spain and the Inquisition. This treatment, like the sufferings of Foxe's Martyrs which were repeatedly published and embellished throughout Elizabeth's reign, spawned the so-called 'Black Legend' detailing Spanish and Catholic atrocities against Protestants abroad, which boded ill for the treatment of native and Catholic converts within England.

Events in neighbouring France and the Low Countries added to such horrors and fears. Relations between Spain and her colony in the Netherlands deteriorated throughout the 1560s, culminating in the nobles' and then the Protestant and national revolt against Spain. The vicious and vigorous counter-measures of the duke of Alva between 1567 and 1573, including the judicial murders of the aristocratic leaders Egmont and Horn and of several hundred other rebels, infuriated English Protestants and led to increasing demands upon Elizabeth to declare herself against Spain.

Likewise, the onset of the French Wars of Religion, and especially the massacres of the Huguenots on St Bartholomew's Eve in 1572, had a profound effect upon English Protestant opinion, not least upon Sir Francis Walsingham, who was stationed as a diplomat in Paris at the time.

Domestic dangers

Plots and conspiracy

Meanwhile, events in Scotland drove Mary Queen of Scots from her throne and into captivity in England. At first supported by the French and increasingly a figurehead for Spanish and Counter Reformation ambitions, she was to be a thoroughgoing nuisance to Elizabeth herself and to the long-suffering privy council, who had to endure long years of Elizabeth's dithering over her cousin's fate.

Virtually from the moment she crossed the border from Scotland, Mary became a focus of plotting and infatuation. She was a focus for the duke of Norfolk's and of Ridolfi's ambitions and schemes from 1568, then of Throck-morton's Plot in 1583 and finally of Babington's Plot in 1586. Although it is common to assess the relative threats posed to Elizabeth's regime by puritan and Catholic, there was a simple difference between the two. Although enthusiastic Protestants were exasperated by and, in turn, exasperated Elizabeth, they were on the same side. Elizabeth found their rudeness, their presumptions upon her prerogatives, their demands for reform and their attacks upon her bishops infuriating and undoubtedly subversive of good order and authority. Yet they were desperate for her to place herself at the head of their schemes and projects. They did not desire her death. In contrast, virtually every plot involving Mary saw Elizabeth's death as a *sine qua non*.

Treason

In 1570, having declared 'Elizabeth to be a heretic', Pope Pius V declared her 'to be deprived of her pretended title to the . . . crown and of all lordship, dignity and

A popular anti-papal woodcut showing the pope as Antichrist 'inspired' by the breath of devils. Anti-Catholic, anti-papal and anti-Spanish propaganda was rife in later-Tudor England. How far was Catholicism a threat to good order and authority? What steps did the Elizabethan government take to counter militant Catholicism?

privilege whatsoever'. He further absolved 'the noble, subjects and people of the
. . . realm from any duty arising from lordship, fealty and obedience'. This official
endorsement of treason against Elizabeth was a virtual declaration of war and
drastically changed the way Elizabeth's government viewed and treated Catholic
subjects.

An Act of 1571 threatened not only those who heeded the pope's call, but
also 'their procurers, abettors and counsellors . . . with the pains of death . . .
and forfeit of all their lands . . . goods and chattels'. Further Acts in 1581 and
1585 followed further provocation in the form not only of murder plots involving
Mary Queen of Scots, but Spanish involvement in the affairs of Ireland,
fomented as early as 1571 by the ubiquitous Ridolfi. There, the Fitzmaurice
Rebellion of 1577 was followed in the 1590s by the effective reconversion of
native Irish to Counter-Reformation Catholicism, and to the highly dangerous
risings of the earl of Tyrone. The latter's success was built on years of Jesuit
missions and waited upon the several Armadas that headed for Ireland after
1588. Only bad luck, bad weather and bad timing ensured that the single
Spanish expedition which made landfall in support of Tyrone in 1601 arrived
too late to achieve victory.

In 1572, Catholic missionary priests were given 40 days to quit the country on
pain of death. This was but one reaction to the work of the Catholic seminary
founded in Douai in 1568 by William Allen and which sent hundreds of such
missionaries across the Channel. By the late 1570s, some 20 such priests were
sent each year, preaching the revitalised Catholic Faith of the reforming Council
of Trent. From 1580, the first Jesuit missions, spearheaded by Edmund Campion
and Robert Parsons, set out.[4]

Torture

Campion and many others became martyrs. They were subject not only to the
protracted horrors of a traitor's execution, but to systematic torture beforehand.
Although the distinguished jurist, Sir Edward Coke, was to claim that 'there is no
law to warrant tortures in this land' he was being disingenuous. We have seen
Cromwell's enthusiasm for its use in enforcing the Henrician Reformation.
Resistance among monks and abbots to the dissolutions of the 1530s had
witnessed use of physical torture, starvation and flogging. The prosecution cases
against Elizabeth's own mother, Anne Boleyn, against Catherine Howard, and
against many other courtly victims of Henry VIII, were procured by use of the
rack, the thumbscrew and the manacle, usually against servants and
commoners.

When Walsingham returned to England and built up what has been described
as the Elizabethan Secret Service, he depended not only upon an extensive
network of spies and informers (including eventually not only Christopher
Marlowe but also his probable murderers) but also upon the use of torture to
break ring after ring of would-be conspirators. Idealistic new converts to
Catholicism such as Thomas Babington were vulnerable in themselves, through
their servants and their associates, as well as through the self-dramatisation and

incompetence of Mary herself. Walsingham, as spy-master, deployed a rack-master, Thomas Norton, whose long career was to include the breaking of the Gunpowder Plot conspirators in 1605–06.[5]

Thus, we find that Elizabeth's regime institutionalised the rack contrary to the letter of the common law. It was a practice eventually halted by the Long Parliament in 1642, stung by the action of Charles I's chief minister, the earl of Strafford. He had reacted to the rioting of the pro-Parliamentary mob by the simple device of racking to death one of the London apprentices involved during the lead-up to the Civil War.

The Catholic dilemma

The policy of Philip II of Spain and of the contemporary papacy wrecked Elizabeth's initial and conciliatory policy towards Catholicism. As Christopher Haigh puts it, 'the old religion was not going to die out – it would have to be murdered'.[6] The work of the seminarists and Jesuits created troublesome new converts. In so doing, a dreadful dilemma confronted the native Catholics, many of whom compromised their civic loyalty by giving shelter to the missionaries and by turning a fatally blind eye to the deeds and words of several generations of conspirators from 1570 to 1605. An estimated 187 missionaries embraced Catholic martyrdom, and the missions themselves utterly disrupted the organic absorption of old religion into new that Elizabeth had hoped for.

Protestants and disorder

After the Throckmorton Plot of 1583 was foiled, the leading citizens of England drew up the Bond of Association, which effectively provided for a Protestant vigilante organisation to take action should any similar plot actually remove the queen. Prominent among the authors were Cecil, Walsingham and Leicester, key figures in the privy council who were acutely aware that they had everything to lose should the queen die.

In a way, the queen was herself responsible for a sense of disorder and instability for she was almost wholly unwilling to pronounce satisfactorily on the succession or upon her matrimonial status.

As long as she failed to name an heir or contract a marriage, there was a gap at the heart of her regime and a standing temptation for Catholic enemies to seek her assassination and overthrow.

Parliament protests

Elizabeth antagonised reform-minded Protestants throughout her reign and, unsurprisingly, many repeatedly registered their anger and their enthusiasm for reform in the Commons. In 1566, at the height of the controversy over the wearing of vestments, Elizabeth was confronted by more than a dozen different plans for a revised Protestant Prayer Book. Two generations of parliament men persevered in bringing in 'a Bill and Book' for consideration before the Commons, yet such efforts were as likely to provide occasion for discussion of more worldly matters of free speech, marriage and the succession.

After Elizabeth came close to death from smallpox in 1562, the next pa
saw the Commons besiege her with requests for a royal marriage or some
settlement of the succession. The notorious Peter Wentworth harassed Elizac
in 1576, 1586 and again in 1593 on these very subjects. Moreover, the
unfortunate John Stubbs suffered punitive mutilation for criticising Elizabeth's
consideration for a foreign marriage alliance with the French duke of Alençon,
her 'little frog', in 1579.

Marriage and succession

Elizabeth had good reasons to avoid committing herself. Mary I's overenthusi-
astic embracing of a foreign and Catholic marriage had highlighted many pitfalls.
It disappointed English candidates, delivered England into unwelcome foreign
commitments and alliances and had dangerous implications for religious policy.
Flirtation with the idea of foreign marriage kept the English nobility and all
possible foreign suitors guessing. Non-commitment, Elizabeth's favoured gambit
in almost any situation, remained a formidable political and diplomatic tool till
long after she was of unmarriageable age and the succession all but declared in
favour of James VI of Scotland.

Its benefits as a policy were, however, far from clear and were outweighed, in
Protestant eyes, by its defects until very late in the reign.

As with her non-commitment to marriage, Elizabeth was outspoken in her
unwillingness to name a successor for the good reasons of personal jealousy on
her part and, more generally, the fear of faction and support for a successor.
Again the defects and dangers of this policy created strains until at least the
death of Mary Queen of Scots in 1587. Yet eventually the queen was able, not
least through her own consummate political abilities to fulfil a role as the Virgin
Queen, and mother of the nation. This worked in terms of public opinion, in
maintaining an equilibrium at court, in dazzling foreign diplomats and in
manipulating an exasperated, but ultimately loyal, privy council.

Document case study

The reformation of manners

7.1 An attempt to control alehouses

From the Act for Keepers of Alehouses to be Bound by Recognisances, 1552

For as much as intolerable hurts and troubles to the commonwealth of this realm doth
daily grow and increase through such affrays and disorders as are had and used in
common ale-houses and other houses called tippling houses.

Source: G. R. Elton, *The Tudor constitution: documents and commentary*, Cambridge, 1982,
p. 477

attempt to control the unruliness of youth

.he Statute of Artificers, 1563

ort term hiring and unemployment leads to] haunting of ale-houses, using of ملawful games . . . cosinages [cheating] deluding of men's wives, daughters, and maidens, procuring them to whoredom and to pilfer for their maintenance . . . [making it necessary to] reform the unadvised rashness and licentious manners of youth.

Source: Paul Griffiths, Adam Fox and Steve Hindle (eds.), *The experience of authority in early modern England*, Basingstoke, 1996, p. 73

7.3 Education

a *A modern historian quotes from a sermon preached by the (exceptionally young) bishop of Gloucester in 1588*

As the Boy Bishop explained in his Childermas sermon at Gloucester in 1558, 'Marry! That is the very thing that is meant in all good education, to discourage youth utterly as touching vice and vicious manners, and to bolden and courage them in all probity and virtue, and vertuous manners'. The means by which this was to be done were not merely sound instruction and worthy example, but also wholesome correction . . . on the familiar grounds that to spare the rod was to spoil the child.

Source: Paul Griffiths, Adam Fox and Steve Hindle (eds.), *The experience of authority in early modern England*, Basingstoke, 1996, p. 53

b *Lawrence Stone, a modern historian, comments on parents' attitude to discipline*

During the period from 1540 to 1660 there is a great deal of evidence, especially from Puritans of a fierce determination to break the will of a child, and to enforce his utter subjection to the authority of his elders and superiors, and most especially of his parents . . . flogging became the standard routine method of punishment for academic lapses for all schoolchildren, regardless of rank or age; secondly a far larger proportion of the population began to go to school, and therefore became liable to this discipline . . . many more schoolboys were poorly motivated to learn, and therefore created disciplinary problems most easily solved by the use of force.

Source: Lawrence Stone, *The family, sex and marriage, 1500–1800*, Oxford, 1977, pp. 116–17

7.4 Public and severe punishment

The fate of five women brought before a church court in June, 1529

[Five women were convicted for being] persons not dreading God nor the shame of this world but continually using the abominable custom of the foul and detestable sin of lechery and bawdry to the great displeasure of Almighty God and to the great nuisance of their neighbours [and were sentenced] to stand under the pillory . . . and from thence to be conveyed to Aldgate and there to be banished the city forever.

Source: Paul Griffiths, Adam Fox and Steve Hindle (eds.), *The experience of authority in early modern England*, Basingstoke, 1996, p. 60

1 What problems for social discipline does 7.1 suggest were posed by alehouses in particular?

2 In 7.2, what was the government trying to regulate in the Statute of Artificers?

3 The emphasis in 7.3a, 7.3b and 7.4 is on public and violent punishment. What effects might such an approach to discipline have had upon a) schoolchildren and b) 'bawdy' women? How important do you think religion was in fashioning these attitudes towards discipline?

Notes and references

1 Christopher Haigh, *Elizabeth I*, London, 1988, pp. 66–68.

2 Penry Williams, *The Tudor regime*, Oxford, 1979.

3 See the essay, 'The Church of England, the Catholics and the people', in Christopher Haigh (ed.), *The reign of Elizabeth I*, London, 1984, pp. 195–221. (Deborah was an Old Testament prophetess and war leader.)

4 Alan Dures, *English Catholicism*, London, 1993, in the Longman seminar studies series deals with the missionaries effectively. Also see Christopher Haigh (ed.), *The reign of Elizabeth I*, London, 1984, pp. 201–03.

5 Antonia Fraser, *The Gunpowder Plot*, London, 1997, pp. 176–79 (popular history but provides detail and atmosphere); see also Alison Plowden, *The Elizabethan secret service*, London, 1991.

6 Haigh, *Reign of Elizabeth I*.

8 Puritanism, the Church of England and the queen's peace

The puritan challenge

Catholicism presented a mortal and immediate threat to the regime from 1570 onwards, with plot or invasion liable to overthrow good order and replace it with civil war and religious massacre. Protestant reformists, however, merely undermined and challenged the assumptions and ambitions of Elizabeth's regime.

In assessing the degree of disorder threatened by 'puritanism' it is as well to remember that the Elizabethan council contained committed Protestants, puritans even, in the form of Leicester, Knollys, Cecil and Walsingham, throughout the crisis years of Elizabeth's reign. Their work and their often brutal methods in fact sustained the regime.

However, there was a fundamental difference between Elizabeth and many of her loyal Protestant subjects. Her approach to the Church of England was thoroughly Erastian. She wanted a state church subordinate to, and supportive of, the regime. The active, educated preaching clergy and the Zwinglian or Calvinist assumptions of many of her reforming clergy were wholly subversive of such a church. So too were the Baptist and Congregationalist assumptions of many other Protestants both inside and outside the church.

What Elizabeth wanted

It is important to remember that Elizabeth wanted preaching largely to be directed along the lines of homilies on loyalty, good order and support of the regime. She approved of vestments, ceremonial and other relics of 'popery' partly as a matter of personal taste, and partly again as practices marking out the status of clergy and liturgy in the interests of discipline and good order. The same considerations underlay her dislike of clerical marriage. Conversely, her Presbyterian or Calvinist critics stood ultimately for theocracy, where the state would be subordinate to, and supportive of, the church as in Geneva and to a lesser extent in Scotland, where the Lords of the Covenant gave Mary Queen of Scots and later James VI such difficulties. As Elizabeth increasingly drove her long-suffering bishops into the front line to uphold her views on discipline and doctrine, so Presbyterianism came to stand for anti-episcopacy. The ultimate logic of this was stated at the Hampton Court Conference in 1604, when Elizabeth's successor, James, angrily equated Presbyterianism with 'No bishop' and hence 'no king'.

Between 1559 and 1604, bishops had become a vital support of the Tudor and Stuart concept of monarchical authority.

Prophesyings and the classis movement

Presbyterians threatened an alternative order, hence one aspect of Elizabeth's opposition to the prophesyings movement of the 1570s. The presbyters who built up networks like the Dedham classis were subverting Elizabeth's church from within, in effect setting up an alternative source of ecclesiastical authority made up of presbyters and senior presbyters, seemingly with the actual sympathy of the puritan-inclined archbishop of Canterbury, Grindal. Meanwhile, apart from the organisation of the movement, the practice of actual and open discussion of the Bible among the congregations was, by definition, subversive of the controlled and disciplined diet of homily and liturgy advocated from loyal pulpits and by episcopal supporters of the regime.

Anabaptists and Marprelates

If the unsupervised discussion of the word of God was threatening in the hands of the Presbyterians of the Dedham classis, it was downright anarchic when espoused by individual congregations and Anabaptists. Herein lay the scandal of the Matthew Marprelate tracts of the late 1580s and early 1590s. A number of shadowy puritan sects such as the Brownists and the Barrowists were driven beyond the confines and disciplines of the church by the ferocious persecution of Archbishop Whitgift. From among them, secret printing presses disseminated the scornful satires known as the Marprelate Tracts, which directly savaged the role of Whitgift and his fellow prelates. In a sense, by 1590, puritanism had nowhere else to go. Reform Protestantism had been driven out of the Church of England. Parliament was loyal if moribund, the classis movement was dead, and prominent, devout, but respectable puritans had largely taken refuge as heads of their households in a form of household puritanism. For radicals, defiance of the regime and secret preaching, Bible reading and the furtive practice of congregationalism were the only alternatives.[1]

Whitgift and conformity

John Whitgift, archbishop of Canterbury from 1583 onwards and member of the council from 1586, enjoyed Elizabeth's particular support. She described him affectionately as 'my little black husband' and charged him with the ruthless enforcement of conformity within the Church of England. For Whitgift, as with Matthew Parker before him, the maintenance of order was a first priority and he enforced the three propositions and expelled recalcitrants from their livings in their hundreds during his years in office. Yet he was an unswerving Calvinist in key points of doctrine, especially regarding Predestination. The point about Whitgift's mission and about Elizabeth's approach to her church was this obsession with power and order.

Neither Calvin nor Knox had especially inveighed against bishops (episcopacy) and neither Whitgift nor Hooker (author of the 1593 *Laws of ecclesiastical polity,* which effectively stated Anglican doctrine at the end of Elizabeth's reign) differed greatly in aspects of puritan theology from these two reformers. However, from the 1560s onwards, Elizabeth required her bishops to enforce a line on order, discipline and dress and maintain a Prayer Book against all attempts to reform any of these elements. The bishops were in a difficult position as Elizabeth shamelessly looted their estates and livings while substantially underendowing each diocese. Simultaneously, she required them to use their position and the church as an institution to work primarily as a prop of the monarchy.

In short, Elizabeth restored and extended her father's use of the church as an institution of political and social control, to uphold her power and sustain good order. Radicals and reformers who offended against that interpretation of the church's purpose paid with their livings, or, in the case of several Barrowists, with their lives.

In fact, the reality of the Anglican achievement by 1603 should perhaps be seen mainly in terms of power and order. The puritan pamphleteer, Thomas Cartwright, suggested that 'there were heaps of people who had cast aside the old religion without discovering the new', and that 'only a remnant of us had truly and faithfully believed'. Patrick Collinson refers to the puritans' 'sense of isolation in a sea of hostile indifference' where puritan 'enthusiasm' could seem offensive to the majority of the population.[2] In other words it seems likely that religious conformity mirrored traditional social and political conformity outside the ranks of religious enthusiasts. As illustrated above, such enthusiasts, if Catholic, were likely to attract the attention of spy-masters and rack-masters, if puritan were liable to fall foul of Whitgift and the Court of High Commission.

Social conformity

Other notable Elizabethans were to fall foul of the 'sea of indifference'.

We have already noted the fate of alleged witches in post-Reformation England and Scotland. Likewise, the vagrant and able-bodied poor were liable to stand out from the labouring masses and attracted official, often brutal, treatment. So too did unmarried mothers. It is interesting to note that authority in London kept its eye not only on Catholic plotters but also upon eccentrics and philosophers. In the court power struggles towards the end of the reign, the eccentricities and offbeat activities of Walter Ralegh, Doctor Dee the astrologer, Christopher Marlowe the atheist, homosexual playwright and spy, and Thomas Kydd the playwright and torture victim, all attracted attention, and worse, from elements of the secret service. Such attentions echo the concern of Cromwell's regime in the 1530s in cutting off, isolating and eliminating sources of opposition or destabilisation. Under both regimes, what strikes one is the painstaking attention to detail of the authorities. Victims as varied as Anne Askew, Elizabeth Barton, sundry obscure Cistercians and the Catholic martyrs, Fisher and More, could not be suffered to live under Cromwell, and likewise impecunious, slightly scandalous entertainers, such as Kydd and Marlowe, were similarly crushed.

Citing these cases lends a greater degree of credence to Lawrence Stone's comment about the harsh natures of the early-modern English. Was this harshness really all a result of overzealous swaddling of babies? More likely the ever-present proximity of possible violence, riot or rebellion bred an understandable sensitivity to all aspects of non-conformity. Authorities and neighbours naturally distrusted unusual behaviour.

Printing and new learning

Discussion regarding treatment of eccentrics, astrologers and nonconformists at last pinpoints the question of printing and its effect upon both order and disorder. The impact of Gutenberg and Caxton was, of course, enormous, most obviously in religious terms. A. G. Dickens was unequivocal on this point, 'Altogether in relation to the spread of religious ideas it seems difficult to exaggerate the significance of the Press, without which a revolution [the Reformation] of this magnitude could scarcely have been consummated.'[3]

There is no doubt that the printing press provided the means for great floods of heretical propaganda that confounded the Catholic establishment and left the papacy continually on the defensive, even when using print to put its own viewpoint. Print fomented religious disorder and, naturally enough, also fomented political disorder. Yet ironically, Christendom had welcomed the invention of print as a gift from God to facilitate the dissemination of the word of God, not least against the unbelieving and threatening Turks.

The press was simply a double-edged weapon in its implications for religious or political authority. As early as the Hunne case in Henry VIII's reign, it was clear that the printing of Lollard tracts undermined Wolsey's clerical authority. Within a few years, Wolsey's effectiveness as Lord Chancellor was clearly inadequate in attempting to stem the tide of heretical literature flowing in from the continent and beginning to appear from native presses. Although this ineffectiveness may have arisen from Wolsey's relatively humane lack of fanaticism, the potential of, and also the dangers inherent in, printed propaganda were made manifest. Wolsey's royal master, with help from Sir Thomas More, was early into print to defend the Catholic Faith against the writings of Martin Luther, and by the 1520s More himself was famously, crudely, profusely, and indeed scatologically, in print to refute Luther's heresies.

Henrician propaganda

Henry learned quickly and, with the help of Cranmer and Cromwell, directed highly effective propaganda in defence of his projected divorce, against the alleged evils of monasticism and clericalism, to advance his own 'reformation' and to blacken its opponents. Conversely, opponents of Henry's policies at home and abroad found voice in print. By the 1540s, Henry was highly alarmed by the increasing availability of the Bible in English translation. The word of God was becoming too readily available and its message virtually impossible to restrict or, more importantly, to control.

Although literacy, even in a lawyerly and more secular age, was relatively restricted, any student of early-modern printing and its impact must take into account not only multiple readership of quite modest print runs but also the importance of the simple virtues of listening. Printed sermons and inflammatory tracts could be delivered aloud.

Tudor tales

More was one of the most interesting of the early practitioners of printed propaganda, partly through his sheer articulacy, and partly through a versatility that made him a highly effective and extremely biased historian of the early Tudors. Thus, while there is compelling evidence to suggest that his account of the murder of the princes in the Tower derived from being peculiarly well-placed to gain credible and informed accounts of surrounding events, nevertheless his depiction of the crook-backed and evil Richard III was dramatic, compelling and largely misleading.[4]

Tudor governments were to deploy such propaganda largely successfully.

Henry, of course, appointed key books such as Erasmus's *In praise of folly* and the *Book of homilies* in each church in the realm to get his message across.

Similarly, and with very lasting impact, Foxe's *Book of martyrs* became a key text in laying the foundation to the Black Legend, to which over the years were added pamphlets and eye-witness accounts of Spanish cruelty to justify Elizabeth's wars against Spain. Students of Shakespeare and Marlowe will also be familiar with the multitude of subtle and not so subtle appeals to anti-popery, English nationalism, and the depiction of the natural hierarchical order of things, most blatantly in the history plays, which culminate in the overthrow of the unnatural Richard III and the triumph of Henry VII. Late in his career, Shakespeare was more or less writing to royal order to please Elizabeth I and James I.

The queen's peace

We have seen the impact of Catholic conspirators and Protestant extremists upon the queen's peace. We now need to examine Elizabeth's record and that of her agents across the country in keeping the peace. Were there still overmighty subjects? How great or how little was the regime's control over them, and how far were the lowlier subjects kept in good order?

A number of eminent historians have, over the years, painted a somewhat contradictory picture of relations between the crown and the nobility, and again between the greater subjects and the middling and lower sort. In particular there are some flatly contradictory statements and pieces of evidence to reconcile.

A more civilised society?

On the one hand, the laws on Livery and Maintenance, and, more to the point, the changes in mustering which had altered the very nature of the feudal host, meant that the gross lawlessness of the later-fifteenth century was gone.

However, there is impressive evidence that Elizabeth's regime was willing to tolerate degrees of aristocratic thuggishness and even murder. In Lawrence Stone's words, 'the retention of bodyguards and the ability to bring out the tenantry in case of need meant the insecurity continued to prevail in many parts of the country'.[5] He accused Elizabeth and her ministers of a 'caution even timidity' as 'striking evidence of the insecurity of their positions. The greater and more influential the nobleman the more warily they trod', he suggests.

Equality before the law

Certainly there was a considerable degree of insecurity on the part of Elizabeth's regime. Indeed, in the draconian penalties that Elizabeth obtained against the lower sort of rebel in the Revolt of the Northern Earls, and in her comparative tolerance of the higher sort such as the duke of Norfolk, the earl of Essex and Mary Queen of Scots, one might well discern a double standard. However, there were very good reasons for Elizabeth's reluctance to outrage royal and aristocratic sensibilities. As with earlier and later regimes she was well aware of the exemplary advantages of very occasional execution of errant, usually murderous nobles. Her father had executed Lord Dacre in 1541 as a clear example that peers were not above the law, Mary's regime had done the same to Charles, Lord Stourton. Elizabeth, albeit reluctantly, was tried beyond patience to eventually execute the three people already mentioned and, as late as the 1760s, the hanging of Lord Ferrers was popularly used to underline the same lesson for all ranks of society.

However, Stone himself acknowledges the 'steady pressure of the central government straining to impose its own rules and to stiffen the local authorities into enforcing the law'. He even suggests that changes in educational roles and contents and 'in occupational habits and in the mental and moral climate of opinion'[6] were working to produce a less sword-happy, more civilised, aristocracy. Given the antics of the earl of Essex, among others, this at first seems doubtful, but something was happening to affect what was and what was not acceptable behaviour at all levels of society.

Popular legalism

Very recent research emphasises that, by the end of the century, 'there is scarcely any evidence that people used physical threats or brutal attitudes . . . to punish each other'. This, at first unlikely statement, makes sense when one examines the rise of a 'popular legalism'.[7] There is plenty of evidence of this development. We have already seen this at work in the enthusiasm of the middling and lower classes, and for that matter the royal regime, for using Star Chamber and the Court of Requests and King's Bench as legal avenues for curbing and punishing errant aristocrats during Wolsey's ascendancy.

Even the brutalities of the witch-craze point up this enthusiasm. The mean and nasty overswaddled and rather horrid people of Stone's social history expressed their nastiness and unneighbourliness in two highly acceptable ways. The first was in mutually agreed and popular collective sanctions like rough music and parish bullying, and secondly by arraigning the witch before the common law to be hanged, and the vagrant, single mother, or delinquent before the parish authorities to be beaten or expelled.

Binding over

The regime may have trodden warily against delinquent but powerful nobles. Most were essential partners of the monarchy and could not easily be disparaged or despatched and, unlike lesser folk, were usually well equipped to lobby on their own behalf, yet 'by 1606 the rate of litigation in the central courts per head of population was higher than it had ever been before or would ever be again . . . The ever clearer judicial supremacy of those central courts . . . was matched by the efforts of monarchs and ministers to oversee and, where possible, improve the administration of justice at all levels.'[8] Thus, through the justices of the peace and in the shires there seems to have been an overwhelming recourse to a device already popular and pervasive in a different way under Henry VII – the concept of 'binding over' to keep the peace. This was used, as we have already seen, as a device for blackmailing potentially subversive aristocrats. Through Henry VII's enthusiasm for bonds and recognisances, it had become a common, flexible and effective way of resolving disputes by legal means by the beginning of the seventeenth century.

Classier solutions

The technique of bonds and recognisances, as Penry Williams has suggested, had 'virtually unlimited applicability' although there was a distinct class nature to the types of action available. Thus, while the petitioning from 'the better sort of people' would lead to the taking-up of a recognisance against those who had offended them which was notably cheaper than pursuing a full indictment through the courts, the simpler and cheaper technique of binding over to keep the peace was more affordable and more often taken up in cases involving yeomen or husbandmen. Furthermore, there is a strong sense that the sublimation of regular conflict of interests in litigation rather than resorting to violence was connected with social prestige. Violence was the mark of the common sort. There is plenty of evidence of this growth in class difference and in the changing aspirations of the middling and upper classes. Meanwhile, a clear indication of the role of this sort of legal action is to be found in the growth of 'unpopular' or malicious legalism. As cases proliferated, suitors brought cases in order to pursue and extend their personal feuding by non-violent means. It is also worth remarking, in the context of religious change as well as in the reform of manners, that the oath-taking involved in binding over introduced a strong sense of spiritual violence as the oath-taker was put in peril of his or her mortal soul.

A gentler gentry

As mentioned in the chapter on 'The Celtic nations', there were long-term trends which seem to have been changing the attitudes and culture of key groups within society. Among the better educated, humanism was a powerful force for restraint, and so too was the new religion. Thus, in endorsing official programmes for the feeding and employment of the vagrant poor, the fierce Secretary of State, Francis Walsingham, described such work as 'necessary . . . and full of piety'. Likewise, Anthony Fletcher has pointed out that Godliness was a frequent motive for the work undertaken by many justices of the peace and other public servants.[9]

Medieval education with its emphasis on chivalric and warrior codes gave way before the influence of humanist scholars like Erasmus and a distinctly different approach to chivalry which increasingly valued peaceful self-assertion and commitment to public office. Office was not so much a source of wealth in the sense that it had been during the dissolutions, but it was a source and vindication of local prestige and power.

There is evidence not only that the aristocracy, who historically had long pursued the maintenance of their honour and status, remained highly sensitive about their 'good name' but that the gentry and middling sort were increasingly likely to value their own good name and to take up litigation to protect it. Herein lies some explanation of the 'immensely increasing volume of litigation'[10] in Elizabeth's reign. It also helps explain the hysterical behaviour of the embattled earl of Essex, who felt his prestige and power base slip away as he lost office and concessions from his queen in the late 1590s. Interestingly, Essex, and several of his peers, showed a marked fondness for duelling, a practice that was on the increase and was deeply disapproved of in the next reign by James I. However, it remained popular within the strictly circumscribed ranks of arms-bearing gentlemen, reaching a peak of slaughter in the Covent Garden of the Restoration. Feuding and affray in a sense became stylised and sanitised in this practice, both protecting the general public from the spill-over from aristocratic feuds but also strongly emphasising the caste difference between duellists and mere yeomen.

Learning and lawyers

Secular lawyers had greatly influenced the administrative aspects of the Henrician and Edwardian Reformations. The dissolutions, meanwhile, led to a large number of educational foundations while the traditional aspects of clerical education were subject to reform and replacement. Although most of the syllabus at school and at the great universities was little changed there was indubitably a 'thirst of noble and gentry families for education' as Penry Williams points out. Williams also remarks that 'the landowning class educated itself for public office and had closed ranks against the low born'.[11] This was a marked feature of Elizabeth's reign where it was no longer possible for a butcher's son to display the kind of social mobility achieved by Cardinal Wolsey. When all but Christopher Hatton became Lord Chancellor after a career in law, and where the key figures within the administrative personnel of the Elizabethan privy council had been similarly trained up, it was clear that the universities and the Inns of Court were an essential part of the route to the top.

This is borne out in the figures. Thus, in 1550 there were 1,150 undergraduates at Oxford, by 1566 there were 1,750 and some 2,000 by the end of Elizabeth's reign. A similar change affected Cambridge, while the 200 attorneys in the two common law courts in 1560 had multiplied by the year 1606 to no less than 1,050. This was in order to cope with an increase which saw King's Bench litigation grow by a factor of eight during Elizabeth's reign. This latter figure of one lawyer per 4,000 head of population is all the more remarkable for its closeness to the estimated 1,200 royal servants who provided about the same amount of government per head.[12]

Means of control

If the nobility and the gentry were studying, if the law was becoming as much a career option as the church had been traditionally, it may have been easier for Elizabeth's regime to maintain or extend certain aspects of political and social control within these key social groups.

Lawrence Stone has maintained that the aristocracy were in fact in a state of decline, partly from external circumstances arising from such events as the Reformation and partly from allegedly deliberate policy from the Tudor monarchs. There is no doubt that the priority of all the Tudors was control, but all were aware that the aristocracy was a vital element in the ability of the monarchy to maintain overall control of the state. If anything, Christopher Haigh has argued, Elizabeth did her best to support rather than diminish her peers. She was certainly lenient towards important peers when they pursued violent feuds such as the quarrel between Oxford and Knyvett from 1582 to 1583. She left her nobles 'massively under-taxed', allowed many to rack up debts to the crown, subsidised the poorer peers and paid for their funerals. In this she followed William Cecil's advice to 'gratify your Nobility and principal persons of the realm to bind them fast to you'.[13]

Haigh points out that 'more peers became councillors than councillors became peers', and there was a consistency in Elizabeth's dealings, for she did restrict the peerage's growth while in her own words 'maintaining their dignity'. There were 57 peers when Elizabeth came to the throne in 1558; there were only 55 in 1603. It was left to James I to reverse this tendency, although to a large extent he was necessarily opening the flow of patronage where his predecessor had stored up trouble and resentment for herself.

Elizabeth allowed only ten new creations in 44 years and those went either to her relatives or those of established peers. She considered, and then rejected, a plan for new creations proffered by Cecil in 1589. Control of the aristocracy was all-important, but there are also signs of great trust between this section of society and the crown.

Arms and the man

We know Elizabeth was tolerant of powerful but necessary peers, and reluctant to punish even the most unreliable. In fact, the ultimate removal of both the duke of Norfolk, and of her own cousin, Mary Queen of Scots, required courts made up largely of trusted peers. Eight earls were present to condemn Mary.

Elizabeth's solicitude towards the nobility does not invalidate Stone's thesis. Her attempts to shore them up may have been insufficient in the context of wider pressures. She did, however, benefit from the thirst for noble service to the regime, and in return employed peers on her council, on special embassies and commissions and, most especially, greatly regularised and extended their functions as regional partners in the government of the realm.

In the crises of 1584 and 1588, it was to the nobility that the privy councillors and the queen turned for political support and for troops. The Bond of Association of 1584 was a bond comprising the lords and deputy lords lieutenants of the shires, almost exclusively made up of the key aristocrats of the realm. In 1588, although the trained bands were summoned, it was the retinues of loyal nobles whom Elizabeth favoured in the Armada crisis.

Retinues and musters

Some of the military problems faced by the earlier Tudors have been briefly touched upon. These ranged from the sheer cost of warfare, something which Elizabeth was more aware of than most, but also centred round questions of quality, quantity and trustworthiness.

While the early Tudors never sought actually to abolish the practice of retaining, the experience of the Wars of the Roses made restraint on the part of the nobility essential. This was something which the combination of statute,

Siege warfare in the early-sixteenth century showing the use of firearms to capture the town. During the Italian wars the cost of warfare became prohibitive for all but the richest military powers. The wars fought by Henry VIII and Elizabeth I late in their respective reigns were cripplingly expensive. How were England's armies raised under the early Tudors? In what ways and for what reasons did methods of mustering and training troops change later in the century?

principally the 1504 Statute of Liveries, and the work of General Surveyors and Prerogative Courts seem to have largely achieved. The Tudors were faced with three possible forms of recruitment. The feudal host, mustered at shire level, was a moribund and highly unreliable resource, whether for home defence against foreign invaders or for the suppression of internal revolt. The embarrassments incurred by successive regimes have been noted right up to the 'watershed' of the 1569 Northern Revolt. However, the gentlemen volunteers and retainers, who made up much, for instance, of Henry VIII's invasion force of 1513, would be expensive, might be untrustworthy and might, indeed, not be made available at all. Yet the third choice, recruitment of foreign mercenaries, much used by Edward's regime and by Mary, would certainly be expensive and would be unpopular, too. It is notable that Elizabeth avoided the third choice.

From 1539, when another invasion scare loomed, the Tudors looked to improve the gentlemen volunteers. Musters were held and information carried over to 1542, as Henry planned his own invasion army. The duke of Northumberland, in 1550, placed lords lieutenants in all counties to be responsible for musters and home defence, although these were allowed to lapse. Elizabeth had recourse to the lieutenancies early in her reign, then on a more systematic basis from 1569, and again when war and Counter-Reformation Catholicism became a virtually permanent threat.

Lords lieutenants

The lords lieutenants of the counties included figures such as Burghley, Knollys, Walsingham and Hatton. Such senior council figures could not be constantly embroiled in local affairs, and so the appointment of up to six deputy lords lieutenants and, beneath them, suitable captains established a major and permanent source of service to the central government by the grandees and a palpable link between central and regional government. With training increasingly a feature of the mustering of these county troops after 1569, it was claimed that a force of 26,000 men were available to resist the 1588 Armada. Perhaps not least of the benefits of the new system was the binding of local grandees to the crown where, again, prestige meant a great deal. The social disgrace of loss of a lieutenancy was not lightly to be undertaken. Furthermore, in Elizabeth's reign the lords lieutenancies, together with the appointment of provosts marshal in key areas, were to provide an important link in the battle to control the disorders and vagrancy common to ports and military zones in time of national conflict.

Notes and references

1 For pre-revisionist accounts of the Church Settlement, see A. G. Dickens, *The English Reformation*, London, 1964, pp. 401–23; and J. E. Neale, *Elizabeth I and her parliaments*, London, 1953. For a more recent account see Penry Williams, *The later Tudors*, London, 1996; and Christopher Haigh, *Elizabeth I*, London 1988, Chapter 2.

2 Patrick Collinson, 'The church and the new religion' in Christopher Haigh (ed.), *The reign of Elizabeth I*, London, 1984, pp. 173–74.

3 Quoted in Elizabeth L. Eisenstein, *The printing revolution in early modern Europe*, Cambridge, 1983, p. 148.

4 Alison Weir, *The princes in the Tower*, London, 1992.

5 Lawrence Stone, *The crisis of the aristocracy, 1558–1641*, Oxford, 1965, p. 222.

6 Stone, *Crisis of the aristocracy*, pp. 234–39.

7 Stone, *Crisis of the aristocracy*, quoting Cynthia Hemp, p. 215.

8 See Williams, *Later Tudors*, pp. 151–52; see also Steve Hindle, 'The keeping of the public peace', in Paul Griffiths, Adam Fox and Steve Hindle (eds.), *The experience of authority in early modern England*, Basingstoke, 1996. Hindle usefully suggests that litigious enthusiasm in the form of the recognisance was arguably crucial to the keeping of the public peace at every social level, pp. 283–39. Similarly, Joyce Youings, *Sixteenth century England*, London, 1984, calls 'vexatious litigation a very effective form of private warfare', p. 223.

9 Quoted in Paul Slack, 'Poverty and social regulation', in Christopher Haigh (ed.), *The reign of Elizabeth I*, London, 1984, pp. 237–38.

10 Williams, *Tudor regime*, p. 428.

11 Penry Williams, *Later Tudors*, pp. 151–52.

12 Christopher Haigh, *Elizabeth I*, London, 1988, pp. 57 ff.

13 Paul Slack, in A. Fletcher and J. Stevenson (eds.), *Authority and disorder in early modern England*, Cambridge, 1985, pp. 12–13. See also A. Fletcher, *Tudor rebellions*, London, 1983.

9 Tudor rebellions

From the moment Henry VII took the crown at the Battle of Bosworth through to Elizabeth's last breath upon her deathbed, all the Tudors faced an ever-present threat of rebellion. Only with hindsight does the Tudor dynasty have an aura of security and permanence for several revolts came remarkably close to success. Furthermore, although the Revolt of the Northern Earls was to be the last major revolt against the Tudor monarchy, Elizabeth's government was not to know that and remained understandably fearful of the threats represented by Catholic plotters, puritan dissidents, and above all from vagrants and the dispossessed.

Early troubles

Pretenders

All the Tudors faced armed rebellions. Henry VII was most obviously vulnerable, given his position as a usurper and as an individual with a very tenuous hereditary claim upon the throne. He was, moreover, only the latest claimant after a long period of wars and commotions. It is a measure of Henry's weakness that he had to defend his throne at the Battle of Stoke so soon after his accession. It is a further measure of his weakness that such credence could have been placed upon the claims of such implausible pretenders as the youthful Simnel and the Burgundian Warbeck. These revolts were essentially part of the Wars of the Roses, a fact that was reflected in the nature of the pretenders' recruits, the Yorkist and foreign backing they received, and by the highly provisional response that Henry's diplomacy, particularly his marriage overtures relating to his sons, received from the French and Spanish kings.

Rebellion in Yorkshire and Cornwall

There were two curious outbreaks of rebellion, one in Yorkshire, the other in Cornwall, which take on a different significance.[1] Firstly, in 1489, there was armed resistance to the collection of the subsidy for that year. The earl of Northumberland was murdered and prolonged rioting had to be suppressed by a force led by the earl of Surrey. Secondly, there was the Cornish Rebellion of 1497, which broke out in resistance to Henry's taxation for his war against Warbeck in Scotland. The commons seem to have been provoked by the increasing sums being raised through subsidy, and the fact that the tax hit the poor proportionately harder than their betters. The rebels mustered around 15,000 men and advanced as far as Blackheath. These outbreaks displayed resistance to aspects of early Tudor government which were to become typical of the regime and which would therefore spark rebellion again.

Tax and heavy-handedness

Thomas Wolsey's vulnerability as the king's first minister may not have been obvious to many of his critics who tended to be both angered and impressed by the cardinal's ostentatious displays of power and wealth. However, when government attempts to raise money for the king's ambitions in the Habsburg–Valois wars in 1525 led to widespread resistance to the so-called Amicable Grant, Henry wisely back-pedalled to cancel the grant. Wolsey was left to endure all the anger provoked by the episode. This was significant for Wolsey, as it underlined his expendability, while the Amicable Grant proved lastingly significant for Henry and his subjects. Above all, the revolt against the Amicable Grant had seen a rejection of government taxation, a rejection in fact of an attempt by the Tudor regime to extend the demands of its government. It had been a successful revolt. Henry had had to retreat and, in doing so, had humiliated his chief minister.

This set a dangerous precedent which was fully comprehended in the rebels' demands in the next great outbreak of revolt – the Pilgrimage of Grace from 1536 to 1537.

Major rebellions

The Pilgrimage of Grace

The Pilgrimage of Grace led the government to lose control of most of England north of the Ribble and the Trent. Faced with no less than nine 'hosts' including the well-directed and idealistic 10,000 pilgrims under the command of Robert Aske, Henry was humiliated into lengthy bargaining with the rebels and only preserved his position through a combination of bluff and bluster.

Whose revolt?

While the facts of the revolt are exceedingly well documented, the interpretation of its causes and support have long been controversial.

G. R. Elton argued forcefully that Aske was a front man for a number of courtiers sympathetic to Catherine of Aragon. They had been displaced by the royal divorce and Act of Succession, and felt cheated that their influence was not restored in 1536 at the fall of Anne Boleyn. Elton played down economic grievances and stated 'it was the gentry leaders, not the commons, who singled out the hated ministers of the crown, and one wonders whether the peasants had ever heard of Cromwell, let alone Rich'. He concluded, 'from the first, the real lead came from the local gentry' who had been 'alienated from the court'.[2]

However, it has been convincingly argued that the revolt would have taken place regardless of any impetus from an Aragonese court faction. Although key leaders such as Hussey, Darcy and Constable had substantial positions both at court and in northern society, their contributions did not account for the sheer scale of a series of risings which took place in Lincolnshire, Lancashire, the West and East Ridings, Cumbria and Durham, nor for the considerable amount of religious imagery displayed by several of the hosts.

Religion or too much government?
The latest major study of the revolt by M. L. Bush picks out much common ground between the different outbreaks: 'Each professed to be a rising of the commons; each was similarly marked by a concern for both the Faith of Christ and the Commonwealth; each hated the government for being extortionate and heretical. All recruited from the whole range of society.'

Bush acknowledges the manipulation of the gentlemen and clergy involved and credits this manipulation with the conversion of broad and deep discontent into a genuinely popular rebellion.[3] A point made by most commentators is the extent of the anger and the rumour-mongering provoked by the sheer level of government activity in the North from 1535 to 1536. Both Fletcher and Elton emphasise the effects of no less than three government commissions active in Lincolnshire immediately prior to the first and unarguably most spontaneous of the risings.[4]

Herein lies a clue not only to this sudden outburst in the middle of the reign of a long-established and successful king in the full flush of adult vigour and ambition. There was a great need for the monarch to be 'kingly' but, in the mid-1530s, a kingly government had become too ambitious, and too far-reaching. Later Tudor governments would similarly try the patience of their subjects.

In the initial Lincolnshire rising, hostility was expressed openly against the king's commissioners, both over the collection of taxes (an echo of the Amicable Grant) and over the dissolutions. Later, the pilgrims' petition demanded 'the reformation of that which is amiss' and 'the punishment of the heretics and subverters of the laws'.[5] Moreover, although commentators have stressed the fact that the pilgrims only re-established 16 of the 65 monastic houses in the North, those restorations and the whole imagery of the Five Wounds of Christ, which appeared on the rebels' banners and badges, highlight the importance of religious grievances to the rebels. Furthermore, both in Lincolnshire and in the Pilgrimage of Grace itself, the rebels emphasised the taking of oaths variously to be 'true to God, the king and the commonwealth' or 'to God, the king and the commons'.[6] The religious element is inescapable, as, of course, it was for Elton's putative Aragonese courtiers who had by definition been sidelined by a royal divorce that required a breach with Rome and all that followed.

Policy and police
The commons, in Lincolnshire and across the North, were subject to the poor harvest of 1535 and the indifferent one of 1536. In some areas they were aggrieved by enclosures and oppressive landlords. Above all, they were struck by the arrival of unprecedented displays of government interference, which impinged directly upon them in the form of tax, in the dissolution of the smaller local monastic houses and, most urgently, in the form of disturbing rumours. The

commons feared the loss of their local church property, further tax demands, and were ripe for agitation by their natural leaders among the priests and gentry. Pilgrims specified their dislike of Cromwell and their affection for the former queen, Catherine. In short, all over the North, the commons were mobilised against the consequences of the Henrician Reformation. Their basic aim, in Bush's words, was 'to persuade the king to dispose of Thomas Cromwell and all that he stood for'.[7] The rebels were rejecting the policy represented by the Henrician Reformation and the whole panoply of 'police' in the form of administrators, commissioners and enforcers that Cromwell had set up to justify, organise and carry out the spoliation of the church and monasteries and to crush any resistance to the Reformation.

Loyal fictions

The fictions commonplace to rebellion have helped confuse the historians. One convention was the insistence of prominent gentlemen that they were waylaid, coerced and convinced into joining the rebellion by the spontaneous acts of the commons. Both Aske and Darcy claimed this, as later on Robert Kett did in justifying his own treason in 1549. Elton is scornful about these claims and tends to dismiss or underplay the degree of spontaneity in the revolt. Furthermore, leaders and meaner rebels usually preserved the fiction that their quarrel was not with the king but with his 'evil counsellors'. This claim was a traditional 'get out' clause to soften the appalling prospect of sinful rebellion, yet there was more to it than mere special pleading. For all the main Tudor rebellions, with the single exception of Thomas Wyatt's revolt against Mary, fell short of attempting to remove the sovereign. Indeed, the rebellions, with the conspicuous exception of the Cornish 'Prayer Book' revolt, were largely bloodless. Aske's Pilgrimage claimed only one life, while Kett's administration of justice over a succession of captives was studiedly moderate. These were polite rebels with limited, or confused, and often wildly disparate shopping lists of demands.

A society of orders

The Pilgrimage of Grace came close to victory. Indeed, in forcing a truce upon the government in October 1536 and apparently negotiating a settlement in December, the rebels showed signs of being unable to comprehend or exploit their level of success. Crucially, their demands remained limited, their spokesman Aske remained credulous and respectful of the king and the duke of Norfolk, and the rebels never stirred southwards, enabling Henry to lull his own court into misleading complacency about the extent of the revolt. In Bush's words, 'the secret of success for the pilgrims had lain in their mobilisation of a huge force'. This was 'not a rabble of peasants; nor were they the retinues of lords and gentlemen'. Aske, inspired by the precedent of the Amicable Grant disturbances, pursued a confident strategy of negotiation backed by the menace of this force. Significantly, as with most other Tudor rebels, he was both loyal and conservative. The leadership and ranks of the rebellion included gentlemen, priests and commons, and 'all three orders believed that the government was showing contempt for the society of order'.[8] In fact, the gentlemen rebels often implied an important truth because they were local and regional leaders who were often genuinely sympathetic to the problems of their poorer neighbours and might, particularly in the context of 'loyal' rebellion, be responsive to the commons' spontaneous demands for action. Their place within the society of orders was to both govern and protect the lower orders particularly against the unnatural government of the 'base-born' Cromwell.

The Western Rebellion

The resistance in Cornwall and Devon in 1549 cannot be separated in a general sense from the overall crisis of the mid-Tudor period. This was genuine violent rebellion that was only suppressed by full-blooded and hard fighting. The veteran Lord Grey described the final battle at Sampford Courtenay as 'as murderous a fray' as he had ever fought in. The last battle may have seen as many as 4,000 rebels killed.[9]

It was a major outbreak. Philip Caramani claims that it was 'the most formidable opposition to the Reformation that England saw'. There was, again, a 'reluctant' leader, Humphrey Arundell, who was, crucially, 'a skilled tactician'. Again, the emphasis was upon the right of subjects to take up arms against a delinquent king and his incompetent or evil counsel. Caramani even argues that this 'right' was implicit in the coronation oath. He also strongly endorses the spontaneity of the Western Rebellion. It was 'a spontaneous expression of the people's piety without any previous plot or planning'.[10]

There is evidence of resentment at the new sheep tax, and a disgruntled disappointment among the poor that, although they no longer benefited from monastic resources and charity, they were still heavily taxed. However, the predominant motive for rebellion seems simply to have been rejection of the new Edwardian Prayer Book and the whole thrust of Cranmer's religious policy. If spontaneous, resentment was nevertheless on a long fuse, with trouble simmering since the William Body incident of the previous year.

Body, 'a stupid, unscrupulous, drunken, bragging brute',[11] was beaten to death in a riot. He was killed as the intrusive and personally unpleasant agent of an unpopular and intrusive programme of government religious policy. As such, his death is reminiscent of the killing of the earl of Northumberland in 1489. His killers were apprehended and, despite a general government pardon, some ten brutally exemplary executions were inflicted. It was into an atmosphere of brooding resentment that the government then chose to intrude the new Prayer Book, its English perhaps not even understood by Cornish speakers. Worse, this was not the confident mature government of the Henrician period, but the newly established, and murkily legal, Somerset administration, already committed to major warfare in France and Scotland, and shortly to be distracted by further rebellion in Oxford and East Anglia.

Kett's Rebellion

Kett's Rebellion in Norfolk, and the associated troubles in Suffolk, contrasted sharply with the almost contemporaneous Cornish revolt. The historian, Land, states flatly that 'the causes of the Norfolk rebellion, and most of the civil disturbances of 1548 to 1549, were economic and social rather than political. Religious doctrine was not a factor in the Eastern Rising'.

Where Cornishmen had brutally despatched Body in 1548 and the unfortunate local magnate, William Hellyons, in 1549, the Norfolk rebels directed their violence largely upon enclosure fences, spared prisoners (not without some frights[12]) and followed a strategy under Kett which was strikingly like that of the Pilgrims under Robert Aske. In other words, the Norfolk rebels sought to negotiate with menaces. They had up to 15,000 in arms against an already overstretched government. Furthermore, given Somerset's sponsorship of the Commonwealth ideas of John Hales, and his approach 'almost to the last that a policy of leniency, conciliation and gradual redress of grievance would obviate the necessity for military action', this strategy seemed realistic. Kett made no move towards London and was content to carry on his pseudo-government on Mousehold Heath outside Norwich for some six weeks.

Class war

Kett was 'primarily a wealthy gentleman farmer' whose confederates were also of a middling sort 'committed to pursuit of a class war from its [the rebellion's] very first days'. Indeed, it has been remarked that in 1549, 'the harmony of Tudor society collapsed and class hostility flared up'.[13] Even in the west, rebels demanded limits upon the number of servants permitted to gentlemen, and the leadership of loyalists conspicuously devolved upon local gentlemen such as Carew, Grey and Russell, who showed a taste for real brutality in suppression of the commons. In the east, enclosure and inflation formed the background to real economic hardship. Of Kett's demands, 17 out of 29 focused on landlords, rents and enclosure. These grievances reflected local feeling, demanded local solutions, and justice dispensed from Mousehold Heath was imposed upon every gentleman that the rebels could arrest and try before the Tree of Reformation.[14]

Like Aske's rebels in Yorkshire, Kett's forces were trying to restore a natural order, to remedy and punish the perceived deficiencies of engrossing, enclosing and uncaring gentlemen. With the removal of Somerset and under the direction of Lord Paget and the earl of Warwick, the ruling class explicitly rejected the sympathetic policies of Somerset and Hales (as their representatives had already done in parliament) and opted for simple repression.

Wyatt's Rebellion

Sir Thomas Wyatt came as close as anybody to overthrowing a Tudor monarch. In Fletcher's words, he was presented with 'a magnificent opportunity'.[15] Yet the rebellion was premature, as it was triggered by the exposure of the details of the plot to the government by its central figure, Edward Courtenay. The plan to marry this distant claimant to the throne to the Princess Elizabeth was revealed, forcing the plotters into hopeless, ill-executed attempts at four co-ordinated regional rebellions.

Of these, only Wyatt's raising of his tenants and the county levies in Kent was remotely successful. Sir James Croft wholly failed to raise Herefordshire, Sir Peter Carew briefly demonstrated in Cornwall before precipitate and panicstricken flight, while the duke of Suffolk abandoned the Leicestershire rising when greeted with outright hostility locally.

These events illustrate just how difficult it could be to raise forces against the crown. The Pilgrimage of Grace had benefited from use of the gentry's own mustering organisation, with the added advantage that genteel leadership and organisation denied the crown its own and only mechanism for enforcing order in the North. Likewise, Wyatt benefited from his own work as a former loyalist in improving the muster in Kent, with defence of the county against France originally in mind.

A close-run thing

Wyatt gained from the proximity of Kent to the capital. The trained bands led by the semi-retired duke of Norfolk failed to put up significant resistance to Wyatt's force of some 3,000 men, many of them deserting to the rebels. Although Wyatt may have approached London overcautiously, certainly giving Mary time to inspire the loyalists and organise the city for resistance, nevertheless the Londoners displayed curious ambivalence towards the rebels as they approached through Knightsbridge. Only at Ludgate was it clear that the city would back the monarch. Significantly, because Wyatt was very much a member of the ruling elite, and had used anti-Spanish propaganda with particular effectiveness, the elite failed to close ranks with the unanimity displayed against the northern pilgrims, the distant Cornish and the commoners of East Anglia. Furthermore, only Wyatt made a realistic lunge for the capital backed by a clear-cut plan to remove Mary and replace her with Elizabeth.

A shaky regime

The major success enjoyed by the core Tudor administration, which was able to service the governmental functions in England throughout the mid-Tudor period, and to emerge substantially unchanged into the Elizabethan era, has been emphasised. Yet without question, that administrative elite could and would have survived, substantially unchanged even if Wyatt had succeeded and brought Elizabeth early to the throne. Few of Mary's ministers would have been sorry to see the Spanish rejected and many of them would have been sufficiently flexible to make their peace with the incoming regime. After all, the long-standing and powerful Henrician regime provoked outrage among its subjects in the 1530s. Moreover, a shakily constitutional Somerset regime took risks with an intrusive and alien religious policy and with an ambiguous social policy, provoking trouble respectively in the west and the east of the country. Undoubtedly, Mary's new regime was pushing its luck, not so much with a policy of Catholic restoration, as with the Spanish marriage and the provocation of those members of the court elite who either felt excluded or feared imminent exclusion. As Fletcher has suggested, the resort to rebellion by the excluded 'arose because of the ineffectiveness of the constitutional methods of opposition to the royal marriage policy'.[16] They very nearly succeeded.

The Northern Rebellion

Otherwise known as the Revolt of the Northern Earls, this episode in 1569 did originally offer a coherent plan to advance a marriage of Mary Queen of Scots to the duke of Norfolk, and possibly to remove Elizabeth, or at the least to dictate religious, succession and conciliar policy to her. Like Wyatt's rebellion, it began prematurely, but, although it briefly left the crown's representative and its government isolated and helpless in the North, it never really threatened success. Like so many other outbreaks, it was local, conservative and defensive. As ever, distance from London lent time and regional credibility, enabling the rebels to assemble forces and enjoy initial impunity. This distance gave the government time to organise effective reaction, while cushioning the regime from the immediate impact that had arisen from the march of Mary's own forces towards the capital in 1553 and of Wyatt's in 1554. Indeed, where Henry VIII had effectively played down the threat of the Pilgrimage of Grace to lull the court into a sense of security, Elizabeth deliberately exaggerated the danger to persuade parliament lavishly to fund the formation of an overlarge army of repression.

Shamed into rebellion

Three women seem to have brought about the Northern Rebellion. The fount of the trouble was, of course, Mary Queen of Scots, who had been expelled from her throne and retained in captivity in England. Her possible marriage to the duke of Norfolk had been mooted in October 1568. This idea was taken up by Elizabeth's favourite, the earl of Leicester, and by the conservatives, Arundel and Pembroke, as part of a plot to displace Cecil at court and reduce the anti-Spanish drift of contemporary policy. The court plot was effectively quashed by Elizabeth, and Leicester himself brought to heel.

Elizabeth, however, had placed her northern nobles in an awkward position. The leading earls, Northumberland and Westmorland, were justifiably sullen at the downgrading of their influence at court and even in their own heartlands. They were, in Penry Williams's words, 'discontented by the intrusion of others into offices that they considered their own by right'.[17] Catholic in religion, their local ascendancy had been broken by Henry VIII, restored by Mary, and once more set aside by Elizabeth. They had plotted with Norfolk, and he with the adventurer and papal agent Ridolfi, yet there were no clear plans and Norfolk's nerve failed him. He fled from court without permission, provoking Elizabeth's liveliest suspicions. Although Elizabeth's northern agent, Sussex, vouched for the earls, his own loyalty was suspect and the queen ordered the earls to appear at court to explain themselves. Here a third female, the formidable Lady Westmorland, a Neville and sister to Northumberland, chided the timorous earls that, 'we and our county were shamed for ever, that now in the end we should seek holes to creep into'.[18] It was enough. The earls revolted. Elizabeth should have left well alone.

Failure to capture Mary

The well-directed core of their plans, the seizure of Mary Queen of Scots, was thwarted by Elizabeth's prompt orders removing Mary further south from Pontefract. The rebels' forces had lunged south for her, but now retired.

Where Sussex could assemble barely 400 horse, the earls gathered some 3,800 foot and 1,600 horse, although the footmen were of poor quality. However, they lacked the Scottish queen, any of the expected support from Lancashire and Cheshire, or any encouragement from the Catholic nobility at large.

The ties of feudalism were crucial in raising this rebellion for there was little money for wages. Religion and hope of plunder were invoked, with the banner of the Five Wounds unfurled at Durham and with Communion tables overturned and English Bibles burned by the rebels.

Hope of foreign help persuaded the earls to play for time but, as the royal host gathered and winter approached, flight to the North followed. Revolt was almost bloodless, with perhaps five killed at Barnard Castle, but Elizabeth's revenge against the commons was ostentatiously bloody. She demanded 700 deaths and got many of them. It had been the act of 'desperate men who felt they had been driven into a corner'.[19]

A watershed

The Northern Rebellion of 1569 can be seen as the last true rebellion under the Tudors. Apart from the English Civil War, which was a somewhat different phenomenon, 1569 was also the last true revolt against the centre before the Monmouth Rebellion of 1685. Purists even argue that 1569 was itself essentially a faction and lordly quarrel with the monarch and harks back to the revolts of 1549. Certainly, as noted, bastard feudalism and conservatism counted for much in 1569.

Paul Slack refers to 'changes in the attitudes of the political elite' and picks out the earlier experiences of 1549 as 'a demonstration that popular disturbance and religious dissidence were too dangerous to tolerate'. Certainly the rash social policies of the duke of Somerset were abruptly repudiated by his erstwhile colleagues. After 1549, the commons were rarely to find the kind of middle-ranking figures such as Aske, Kett and Wyatt to lead them – that is, gentlemen up to and including peripheral courtiers. Most disturbances of Elizabeth's reign owed their origin either to foreign and religious intrigue, for example Ridolfi, Throckmorton and Babington; or to the leadership, indeed desperation, of factious magnates, for example the Northern Rebellion or the Essex Rebellion; or in 1596 to the sad case of a handful of starving and disgruntled commoners.[20]

The end of the magnates

The northern counties and the magnates who controlled them had long been a source of uneasiness to all monarchs. From 1536 to 1537 in the Pilgrimage of Grace, the North had proved dangerous indeed to the regime and its plans. However, the North fell into abeyance in the mid-Tudor period, at least as a base for revolt. By 1559, however, we find Cecil interrogating Ralph Sadler for rumours and intelligence regarding the North, while in 1565 Mary Queen of Scots trusted the North to rise because its nobility were 'all of the old religion'. Sure enough the revolt of 1569 re-emphasised the dangers of excluding or downgrading any group of the nobility. As Fletcher points out, Elizabeth had deliberately built up the gentry clientele of Northumberland's rival, Sir John Forster, and had put her cousin, Lord Hundson, in charge of Berwick and the East March. Trouble arose not only from Northumberland's resentments, from the ambitions and fears of the duke of Norfolk, and from those of Westmorland, but also derived some impetus from the intrigues of the group of anti-Cecil councillors including Winchester, Arundel, Pembroke and even Leicester.

Once the revolt was crushed, Elizabeth again trusted her cousins and clients, but a combination of flight, exile, death and attainder had at last broken the power of the northern magnates.

Two late rebellions

These last two examples dramatically illustrate how far the Elizabethan regime had come, and point to certain truths about Tudor rebellions.

The 1596 Oxford Rising demonstrated the puny nature of any challenge from the commons during the grim nineties, a decade of starvation and disease. The handful of rebels were inspired by class-based anger and hostility and uttered threats specifically against the rich. They were crushed by the overwhelming and, indeed, disproportionate forces of the state. Military force, torture and the death sentence were brought to bear. As in her sanguinary demands after the Northern Rebellion, Elizabeth, who might dither long and loud over the fate of an errant nobleman, insisted on the most savage of punishment for the commoners who had challenged the order of things.

The earl of Essex was driven by different pressures. Again, his revolt as such was a pathetic, isolated and hopeless affair, where the erstwhile royal favourite despaired, lacking as he did income, office or a credible future at court. His small number of faithful retainers and hopeful adventurers were easily swept away by crown forces and he posed no real threat to the queen at all.

The two outbursts were small scale, their supporters isolated from a bemused populace yet, particularly in the Oxford Rising, we see a hypersensitive regime deploy overwhelming force. In fact the long years of Spanish intrigue and Catholic plotting justified the regime's sensitivity, while the experience of those years had clearly led the regime to arm itself with the spies and the troops to counter any danger. By the end of Elizabeth's reign, order clearly had the measure of disorder, although the Essex disturbance also starkly highlighted the dangers in Elizabeth's methods of favouritism, court appointments and patronage. This danger was further underlined in her last parliaments where monopolies presented an easy target for critics of the regime.

Who were the rebels and what did they want?

It has been said that the Northern Rebellion was 'strikingly non-feudal'. Nine-tenths of the rebels were not tenants at all, although this fact must be balanced by the fact that 'the strength of the rebel army lay in their horsemen', described as 'gentlemen and their household servants and tenants'. If these latter made up the quality among the rebel forces, it was the common quantity who were hanged and suffered after the revolt.

Paul Slack states that 'it was not the very poor who were the participants in major risings, let alone the leaders'. There was in fact a distinct lack of all but the most incoherent of class consciousness to be found in the utterances of most rebels. All held fast to the convenient myth of bad counsel, arguing that king or queen simply needed more honest, more patriotic or more moderate counsel. Indeed, the demands and plans of all rebels were usually moderate and often confused. Only the Wyatt Rebellion seemed specific in its aims to remove Queen Mary, while all others sought marriages, for example between Mary and Norfolk; restorations, such as that of Catherine of Aragon; or religious, social or economic concessions, which was true of almost all of them, with the exception of Essex's madcap affair.

Yet the regime feared the poor. In Francis Bacon's words, the vagrant poor embodied 'a burthen, an eye-sore and a scandal'.[21] They were 'a seed of peril and tumult in a state'. Furthermore, they were perceived to be at their most dangerous in times of dearth. As Cecil observed, 'there is nothing will sooner lead men into sedition than dearth of victual'.[22] The final chapter will show how Elizabeth's regime, working through parliament, lords lieutenants, provost marshals, justices of the peace and church and parish authorities, actively extended government responsibilities and sought to control and defeat that 'seed of peril and tumult'.

A question of leadership

We have seen that dearth and taxes were not incidental to revolts. The events of 1536 and 1549 make this clear. Also, although it was not always easy to mobilise the commons to revolt, religious appeals, hopes of plunder and actual wages could make a difference. Moreover, the frequency of affray and riot at local level suggests the omnipresence of common resort to violence which could be channelled by unscrupulous and ambitious local leaders. There were, too, clear examples of leaderless spontaneity, most obviously in Lincolnshire in early October 1536, in Norfolk and Suffolk, before Robert Kett took his initiative, and in the western murder of William Body, and the subsequent tumults of 1549.

The 'middling sort' played an important role in the Pilgrimage of Grace, in the 1549 revolts, and it is important to note the major impetus Wyatt's Rebellion received from the gentry of Kent. Crucially, they might invoke the mustering organisation on which the Tudor regime depended. Certainly, they could both reflect and mould the commons' anger.

After 1569, these potential leaders are conspicuous by their absence. The Oxford rebels of 1596 were all commoners while the leaders of Essex's tumult were adventurers and courtiers. Yet violence, tumult, anger and dearth continued to mark the commons.

Other channels – a stronger regime

Two Tudors learned from experience. Henry VIII was shaken by the Pilgrimage of Grace. He moderated his religious policy, eventually removed Cromwell, and was careful to remodel the Council of the North and to limit the power of the northern magnates. Elizabeth, whose policy towards her Catholic subjects was generally sensitive, was also careful with her nobility and benefited from the cautious loyalty that many of the Catholic nobility showed in 1569. After 1569, she also benefited from public acceptance of the Black Legend and increasing solidarity against foreign and Catholic treason and plot. When dearth returned in her last years, hers was a long-established, generally wise and sensitive regime, unlikely to repeat the clumsinesses that Tudors had offered in 1536, 1549, 1554 and 1569.

After 1569, the potential leaders of rebellion, whether magnates or gentry, were moving away from violence and were more effectively entwined into the patterns of county and shire administration. As their 'manners' improved they worked to reform the manners of the meaner sort, and through Poor Law administration and food doles sought to contain the worst effects of dearth and vagrancy. As Fletcher has hinted, channels for the expression of gentlemanly resentment at royal policy became better established and more effective as strikingly displayed, for instance, in the debates of the 'Monopoly' parliaments of Elizabeth's last years. Rebellion became very much the last resort of the isolated and powerless.

Document case study

The survival of Roman Catholicism in the North

9.1 The causes of the Northern Rebellion

Sir Ralph Sadler, a senior privy councillor, to Sir William Cecil, 1569 (letter)

I perceive Her Majesty is to believe that the force of her subjects of this country should not increase, and be able to match with the rebels; but it is easy to find her cause. There are not ten gentlemen in all this country that favour her proceedings in the cause of religion. The common people are ignorant, superstitious, and altogether blinded with the old popish doctrine.

Source: A. Fletcher, *Tudor rebellions*, London, 1983, p. 128

9.2 Who rebelled?

A modern historian reflects on the nature of the support for the rebellion

The appeal was quite successful in Durham and north Yorkshire, given the time of year: five or six thousand rebels flocked to the banners of St Cuthbert and the Five Wounds of Christ, and in many parishes the Bible and Book of Common Prayer were desecrated and altars restored . . . the rebellion was strikingly non-feudal: nine tenths of the known rebels were not tenants of the leaders (which is not surprising, as the rising took place away from the Neville and Percy heartlands), and there was much more of a popular movement than has been supposed.

Source: Christopher Haigh, *Elizabeth I*, London, 1988, p. 54

9.3 The arrest of Edmund Campion

Around November 1580, Edmund Campion writes to Dr William Allen saying that he feels the secret police are closing in on him

I cannot long escape the heretics, they have so many scouts . . . threatening edicts come forth against us daily, yet we have escaped thus far; men neglect their own safety to take care of mine . . . They brag no more of their martyrs, since now, for a few apostles and cobblers of theirs turned we have bishops, lords, knights, the old nobility, flower of the youth, noble matrons, and innumerable of the inferior sort either martyred or dying by imprisonment.

Source: *Calendar of state papers domestic additional, 1580–1625*, pp. 24–25, quoted in Alan Dures, *English Catholicism, 1558–1624*, London, 1988, pp. 91–92

Document case-study questions

1 What does 9.1 tell us about the survival of Catholicism in England up to 1569?

2 Does 9.1 indicate anything about Elizabeth's awareness of the need to rule by consent?

3 What is the significance of the reference to the 'Five Wounds' in 9.2?

4 Why does the author in 9.2 make a point of the 'non-feudal nature' of the 1569 rising?

5 Briefly compare and contrast Campion's mission in 9.3 with the events of 9.1 and 9.2.

6 From all these documents and from your own knowledge, say in what ways you think the Catholic 'threat' had grown and in what ways diminished between 1569 and 1581.

7 Use the above documents, and your own knowledge of the Northern Rebellion and other Tudor risings, to describe the differences and the similarities between the 1569 rising and the others.

Notes and references

1 See A. Fletcher, *Tudor rebellions*, London, 1983, pp. 9–12.

2 Quoted in John Fines, *The Pilgrimage of Grace*, London, 1986, p. 7; and see also G. R. Elton, *Reform and Reformation*, London, 1977, pp. 260–72.

3 M. L. Bush, *The Pilgrimage of Grace*, Manchester, 1996, p. 7.

4 Fletcher, *Tudor rebellions*, p. 17; and Elton, *Reform and Reformation*, p. 260.

5 Bush, *Pilgrimage of Grace*, p. 9.

6 Bush, *Pilgrimage of Grace*, p. 12.

7 Bush, *Pilgrimage of Grace*, p. 410.

8 Bush, *Pilgrimage of Grace*, pp. 407–09.

9 Philip Caramani, *The Western Rebellion*, Tiverton, 1994, pp. 90–92.

10 Caramani, *Western Rebellion*, p. 20 and p. 35.

11 Caramani, *Western Rebellion*, p. 13.

12 John Sturt, *Revolt in the West*, Exeter, 1987, p. 49; Fletcher, *Tudor rebellions*, pp. 57–88.

13 S. Land, *Kett's Rebellion*, London, 1977, p. 43 and p. 49; Fletcher, *Tudor rebellions*, p. 98.

14 Fletcher, *Tudor rebellions*, pp. 120–23; Land, *Kett's Rebellion*, p. 67.

15 Fletcher, *Tudor rebellions*, p. 73.

16 Fletcher, *Tudor rebellions*, p. 76.

17 Penry Williams, *The later Tudors*, London, 1996, p. 256.

18 Williams, *The later Tudors*, pp. 256–57.

19 Fletcher, *Tudor rebellions*, p. 92.

20 Paul Slack, *Poverty and policy in Tudor and Stuart England*, London, 1988, pp. 100–01.

21 Slack, *Poverty and policy*.

22 Paul Slack in A. Fletcher and J. Stevenson, *Authority and disorder in early modern England*, Cambridge, 1985, pp. 12–18.

10 The flowering of the Elizabethan state

It is clear that Elizabeth sought to uphold the status of her nobility, and both nobility and gentry sought greater and more secular opportunities in and through education. Also, the religious changes and the rise of national and household puritanism had a marked effect upon concepts of order and discipline and upon the obtaining of these virtues within Tudor society.

Just as the puritan patriarch held sway within his household microcosm, Elizabeth took up the trail blazed by Cranmer, Cromwell and Henry VIII in publicising homilies and the English Bible itself to the congregations of the Church of England where, in Penry Williams's words, 'the most important vehicle for exhorting people to obey the law was the pulpit'.

Furthermore, the apparent decline of true rebellion and personal violence has been noted. We have also seen a rise in litigation which became a route to satisfaction particularly favoured by husbandmen and yeomen upwards to the gentry and even the nobility. Many sources point to the growing gap between genteel, male and educated subjects, and the mass of women and uneducated men and youths. Anthony Fletcher points out 'the gentry so manifestly detaching themselves in manners and values' from the mass of people.[1]

Ruling class views of the poor

This detachment, perhaps a retreat into the household among certain families – the contempt of the lettered for the unlettered – seems to have coloured ruling-class views of the poor and of the danger they posed to society and to good order. If true rebellion was a thing of the past (albeit the very recent past), riot was ever-present, particularly in the recurrent years of dearth which afflicted Elizabeth's reign. Moreover, casual violence among the commons and in the form of footpad theft were viewed, whatever the reality, as much on the increase.

Although some rioting had a ritual, almost acceptable and certainly cathartic quality to it, what Paul Slack paraphrases from a seventeenth-century rioter as 'ambivalent like an episode of rough music – a harmless pastime but in some sort necessary',[2] food riots and urban disturbances in an era devoid of a police force were frightening and were perceived, whatever the reality, as potentially significant. One only needs to recall the massive overreaction to the Oxford Rising of 1596 to appreciate the alarmist thinking of respectable folk in general and of the authorities in particular when dealing with a disturbed commons.

We have already witnessed the alarm spread by the apparent rise in vagrancy during Cromwell's time in the 1530s and again in the mid-Tudor period, when hunger and economic and social dislocation were self-evident. Although the economy stabilised at first in Elizabeth's reign there were distinct and actual rises in both crime and destitution which predictably coincided with bad harvests and economic depression. Penry Williams, in fact, picks out 'three sudden increases, each coinciding with a rise in food prices', the most dramatic coming from 1596 to 1598. Such developments were generally accompanied by an increase in the authorities' enthusiasm for draconian solutions to both problems, an attitude which was compounded by the unfortunate and erroneous assumption after 1569 that it was vagrants who had been largely responsible for the Northern Rebellion of that year.[3]

The vagrant or rogue was certainly an obvious scapegoat for contemporary ills. 'Rogues', 'sturdy rogues', 'bawdy baskets' and 'cutpurses' were angrily denounced by Elizabethan commentators although, as Slack points out, 'the picturesque or professional rogue appears to have been the exception not the rule'. However, there was a good deal of habitual criminality for which vagabonds were responsible and some evidence that levels of criminality did rise, particularly in the 1590s. There were more of them, too, judging from the figures of the London Bridewell, wherein the 60 vagabonds passing through in the year 1560 to 1561, became 204 from 1578 to 1579, and 555 from 1600 to 1601. If there were more rogues, then more crime and more bastardy would follow.[4]

Coercion

Government was sensitive to all sorts of threats and increasingly took on new powers and sought to stop loopholes in the constant struggle to eliminate enemies of good order. A significant aspect of the Reformation had been the gradual elimination of traditional sanctuaries, while benefit of clergy was severely restricted by two acts of 1532 and 1540.

The use of torture has already been noted, but at a more mundane level the privy council actively pursued all aspects of loose talk, and punished rumour-mongering with whipping, pillorying and mutilation. By 1594, such efforts were backed by a statute specifically against the spreading of false rumours.

Times of war and times of dearth increased the urge to coerce, and the willingness to appoint suitable authority with suitable powers. Key figures were the justices of the peace and the local provost marshals, the latter operating effectively in 'military zones' which effectively came under martial law. From 1558 onwards, the provost marshals had specific powers to execute vagrants. Although these figures disappeared during the 1560s, they were restored in 1570 and were appointed to each county in 1588. After the Essex rebellion, marshals were instructed to 'ride the highways' around London to eliminate the disaffected. Again we get a picture of an almost paranoid government.[5]

Poor Laws

Meanwhile, 1563 saw an act 'for the Relief of the Poor' which went further than

1552 in adding compulsion of poor relief contributors to the exhortations required by the earlier act. The troubled time of 1572 saw an act 'for the Punishment of Vagabonds' but significantly 'for the relief of the Poor and Impotent' which made explicit the moral divide between deserving and undeserving poor and promised whipping, boring of the ear and compulsory servitude to convicted vagabonds, with the threat of felony charges on the second and third offence. Although Paul Slack has pointed out that perhaps one vagabond in ten was actually whipped, the case of Joan Wynstone before the Middlesex sessions in 1576 saw this unfortunate woman whipped and branded in February, placed in servitude to her husband in July and sentenced to hang in October. In the previous three years sessions five other Middlesex vagrants had received the death sentence.[6]

The crisis of the 1590s

A pattern had been set of coercion and relief. An act of 1576 'for setting the poor to work' provided stocks of wool for the unemployed to work and set up houses of correction for the defiantly idle. Until the 1590s much of the burden for overseeing this system and for assessing the contributors to the poor rates was in the hands of the justices of the peace. These figures had become veritable maids of all work as they were burdened by 'stacks of statutes' and were increasingly directed by 'a major Elizabethan innovation' in the form of Books of Orders issued to them by the central government. The issue of plague orders in 1578 and dearth orders in 1586 spelled out their responsibilities. It was the justices who had to work with local authorities and, from 1565, with specifically appointed 'commissioners for the restraint of the grain trade' to ensure adequate stocks of food for the destitute. Ironically, however, the price control was dropped temporarily in 1593 'because of the great plenty and cheapness of grain', just in time for a run of four appalling harvests.[7] The commissioners were a by-product of the government's concern to crush contemporary piracy, but the maintenance of food supplies had clearly become an end in itself and their commissions had been regularly renewed after 1565. From the winter of 1586 to 1587, the justices of the peace were under standing orders from the council to supply markets in time of need.

New laws

The justices were also responsible for decisions on the care of all orphans within their jurisdiction, and had also, since the 1563 Statute of Artificers, been required to set and enforce standard wage levels for common occupations. It was not until the Poor Laws of 1597 to 1604 that some of their burden was relieved. Then, at last, overseers of the poor were appointed to each parish, with joint responsibility with churchwardens to provide work, give relief, compel contributions and provide habitations for the disabled. Even then, the justices continued to administer the 1597 Act 'for the punishment of Rogues, Vagabonds and Sturdy Beggars', providing for houses of correction and adding exile to the possible fates of the incorrigible rogue.

A woodcut depicting famine. The Tudor and early-Jacobean regimes were afflicted by episodes of serious famine, notably in the mid-Tudor period, in the 1570s and again in the 1590s. In what ways was simple repression inadequate in confronting poverty?

Elizabethan commissions

The Elizabethan regime worked the justices hard and they responded well, unpaid but active in the interest of their local power and prestige, and of their all-important good name. Meanwhile, the regime built on earlier precedent. Elizabeth used the ecclesiastical commissions that Cromwell had revived to enforce her church settlement. She also appointed special commissioners for the suppression of piracy and for the maintenance of the grain trade. A further commission of 1565 to 1566 was appointed to investigate levels of enclosure and engrossing which was repeatedly blamed by many theorists for both food shortages and rural depopulation.

In the latter, she was working within a tradition established under Wolsey in 1517 and taken further by the duke of Somerset in 1548 to 1549. James, too, investigated enclosures and engrossing in 1607. Parliament, meanwhile, issued 'stacks' of statutes, as the justices complained.

Tillage Acts of 1563 and 1597, for instance, attempted to legislate against rural problems and for the maintenance of arable land. The Statute of Artificers sought to fix wages and status in occupations, making the giving and receiving of excessive wages an offence, as was refusal to work. Sumptuary legislation continued to occupy parliament in the first half of Elizabeth's reign. Yet after 1576, the statutes of Elizabethan parliaments show a significant change of emphasis.

Regulation of the poor

The moral distinction between deserving and undeserving poor was crucial. Thus, in 1571, the city authorities of Norwich inveighed against the slippery slope 'from idleness to drunkenness to whoredom to shameful incest and abominable life, greatly to the dishonour of God and ruin of the Commonwealth'.[8] There was a puritan distaste for the vagabond and for the bastard. After 1576, it showed in the law. The Poor Law, says Slack, was 'not designed as an economic regulator, but as a moral, social and political one'. Reform of manners was 'a striking feature of parliamentary activity between 1580 and 1660', and he details 35 bills on drunkenness, inns and alehouses, nine on Sabbath breaking, nine on bastardy and six on swearing between 1576 and 1610.[9] The reform of the poor was borne out in Quarter Sessions where the punishment of the parents of bastards became one of the commoner entries in the records, and also in royal proclamations where, up to 1581, six out of nine related to clothing worn and after 1581 ten out of thirteen related to vagrancy. The elite, no doubt, immersed in self-improvement, litigation and the new education, could take care of themselves.

Problems and solutions

The Elizabethan regime was sorely tested by plots and disturbances within the realm and by the threat of encirclement and invasion from without. At different times, both the French and the Spanish Empires threatened, while the possibility of religious disorder was a constant for much of the reign. As in the mid-Tudor period, dearth, plague, rural depopulation, vagrancy and trade depression at times tested the maintenance of the queen's peace throughout the realm.

To cope with these problems, Elizabeth expanded the role of government. Her parliaments concerned themselves with all aspects of political, religious, social and economic well-being. They nagged the queen about religion, the succession and marriage. At the end of the reign they picked upon inadequacies and abuses in royal appointments and patronage. She, meanwhile, streamlined her council, while key figures within that body took on more clerks and agents and created a shadowy network of spies and informers going beyond even Thomas Cromwell's efforts of the 1530s. The nobility were co-opted as providers of troops and as lords lieutenants better to govern the regions. They were powerful as patrons of members of parliament, as members of the House of Lords and as local partners in government. They were drawn to court and the games and intrigues of court, but key counsel and administration now devolved increasingly to the professionals.

By 1600, there were some 1,200 royal officials at work, 600 in the household, some 600 others, perhaps one to every 4,000 in the population, a figure remarkably matched by the growth in the number of common lawyers.

The growth in litigation suggests one major way in which the maintenance of good order became easier as gentry and nobility themselves became more orderly. For instance, the Council in the Marches of Wales, formerly swamped by criminal cases, found by the late-sixteenth century that it was dealing mainly with civil cases. The great magnates were gone or tamed, and parliament, priests and puritans worked to mend the manners of the common people.

Yet dearth, vagrancy and the need to combat new threats such as piracy and foreign invasion led Elizabeth's regime to innovation – appointing lords lieutenants, extending the burden upon overworked justices of the peace and appointing commissions on food supplies, piracy, church matters and enclosure. Evidence suggests that private charity had recovered from the Reformation to reach former levels by the end of the century. Even so, the government and local authorities, with the latter usually in the lead, accepted a government obligation to find work and raise money for the relief of the deserving poor. Again, following a moral line, they also sought to reform and punish the idle. By 1603, Scotland and Wales were quiet, the government more effective, the church established. Order rather than disorder reigned, with the defiance of such as the Oxford rebels and the Essex retainers marked by their isolation and the puzzlement of the many. For the Catholic missionary priest and his converts and even for the notorious rogue, a regime happy with the use of torture brought exposure and retribution. In hamlets and villages across the land, rough music, scolding and thrashing punished the shrews and scapegoats or beat submission into the young and the subordinate while in thousands of small commonwealths the father of the household led prayers and crushed dissidence.

Yet, as was remarked about Henry VIII, there were straws in the wind for Tudor authority. The great king had squandered a priceless store of wealth in the 1540s and, although Elizabeth's financial servants, Gresham and the great Chancellor Winchester, stabilised and maintained her fortunes up to 1572, there was a deep conservatism in Elizabeth and Cecil's approach to crown finances. Crown estates were scandalously undervalued and underexploited thereafter and it was others' estates that became enriched and led the way. Despite Elizabeth's personal meanness and her sensible avoidance of warfare, she was drawn into a disastrously expensive Irish conflict which showed Elizabethan administration at its worst and stored up trouble for generations to come.

The Receipts controversy of 1562 to 1597 saw 'the Queen's direct commands [rendered] . . . completely ineffectual for decades at a time'[10] in the Exchequer, and both the Essex affair and the Monopolies Parliaments, at the end of her reign, showed that Elizabeth's system was creaking. It was held together partly by the reflection of past glories, by the queen's own charisma and skill and by the awareness of a new reign and new opportunities around the corner. The travails of the early Stuarts were to reveal how much, despite the new administrators and the partnerships between central and local government, and the commissions and the justices of the peace, still depended upon the skills of the monarch at the apex of power.

Document case study

Rogues and repression

10.1 A rogue

Thomas Dekker described a typical rogue in his Bell man of London: A discovery of all the idle vagabonds in England, *1608*

A rogue is known to all men by his name, but not to all men by his conditions: no puritan can dissemble more than he, for he will speak in a lamentable tune and crawl along the streets, (supporting his body by a staff) as if there were not life enough in him to put strength into his legs . . . Another set there be . . . called STURDY ROGUES: these walk from county to county under colour of travelling to their friends or to find out some kinsman.

Source: John Pound, *Poverty and vagrancy in Tudor England*, London, 1971, p. 98

10.2 A Fagin figure

William Fleetwood, the Recorder of London during the 1570s and 1580s, to Lord Burghley (letter)

One Wotton, a gentleman born and sometime a merchantman of good credit, who, falling some time into decay . . . reared up a new kind of life . . . there was a schoolhouse set up to learn young boys to cut purses . . . note that a foister is a pickpocket and a nipper is termed a pickpurse or cutpurse.

Source: John Pound, *Poverty and vagrancy in Tudor England*, London, 1971, p. 99

10.3 Repression

From the Vagrancy Act, 1531

If any man or woman being whole and mighty in body and able to labour having no land, master, nor using any lawful merchandise . . . whereby he might get his living . . . be vagrant . . . arrest the said vagabonds and idle persons and to bring them to the Justices of the Peace . . . to be tied to the end of a cart naked and be beaten with whips.

Source: John Pound, *Poverty and vagrancy in Tudor England*, London, 1971, p. 103

10.4 The role of justices of the peace

Sir Thomas Smith, writes in his book, De republica Anglorum, *1565*

At first they were but four, after eight, now they come commonly to thirty or forty in every shire, either by increase of riches, learning, or activity in policy and government . . . for the repression of robbers, thieves and vagabonds, of privy complots and conspiracies, of riots and violences, and all other misdemeanours in the commonwealth the prince putteth his special trust . . . also upon suspicion of war, to take order for the safety of the shire, sometimes to take musters of harness and able men, and sometimes to take order for the excessive wages of servants and labourers, for excess of apparel, for unlawful gamers, for conventicles and evil orders in alehouses and taverns, for the punishment of idle and vagabond persons, and generally, as I have said, for the good government of the shire.

Source: G. R. Elton, *The Tudor constitution: documents and commentary*, Cambridge, 1982, pp. 468–69

Document case-study questions

1 What does 10.1 tell us about contemporary perceptions and fears about 'rogues'? Why was there a lack of sympathy for the rogue?

2 There were many 'masterless' children as well as men, partly due to the rise in population. Do you think this sort of comment might prejudice people, making them less tolerant towards children and the poor? Explain your answer. How do 10.1 and 10.2 link with the details in documents 5.1 to 5.4?

3 How far does the treatment of the vagabond prescribed in 10.3 stem from comments about rogues in 10.1 to 10.2? How effective do you think such treatment would have been?

4 What does 10.4 tell us about the role of the justice of the peace in Tudor social legislation? How attractive do you think a repressive role was likely to be for the average justice?

Notes and references

1 A. Fletcher and J. Stevenson (eds.), *Order and disorder in early modern England*, Cambridge, 1985, p. 15.

2 Paul Slack (ed.), *Rebellion, popular protest and the social order in early modern England*, Cambridge, 1984, in the Introduction, p. 12.

3 Penry Williams, *The later Tudors*, London, 1996, p. 190. See also Joyce Youings, *The sixteenth century*, London, 1984, p. 218, in which she states that 'none of the major resorts to arms was directly occasioned by dearth of food'.

4 John Pound, *Poverty and vagrancy in Tudor England*, London, 1971, pp. 97–99; Paul Slack, *Poverty and policy*, London, 1988, pp. 90–97.

5 Penry Williams, *The Tudor regime*, Oxford, 1979, pp. 189 ff.

6 Pound, *Poverty and vagrancy*, p. 47.

7 Williams, *Tudor regime*, pp. 172–90.

8 Paul Slack, 'Poverty and social regulation,' in Christopher Haigh (ed.), *The reign of Elizabeth I*, London, 1984, p. 238.

9 Slack, *Poverty and policy*, pp. 103 and 130–31.

10 J. D. Alsop, 'Government, finance and the exchequer', in Christopher Haigh, *Reign of Elizabeth I*, London, 1984, p. 121.

Select bibliography

The detailed notes and references with each chapter should be studied for the many leads into studies covering each chapter area. For further reading the following are recommended.

High politics and administration

For the so-called New Monarchy, and the reigns of the Yorkists, J. A. F. Thompson, *The transformation of medieval England, 1350–1529*, London, 1983; and J. R. Lander, *Government and community, 1450–1509*, London, 1980, provide good background, while R. Lockyer, *Henry VII*, London, 1990; and David R. Cook, *Lancastrians and Yorkists: the Wars of the Roses*, London, 1984, provide useful sources and discussion of the crown's recovery from civil war. See also S. B. Chrimes, *Henry VII*, London, 1972. See also the two books by C. E. Ross, *Edward IV*, London, 1974 and *Richard III*, London, 1981.

In dealing with Henry VIII's long reign several of the works of G. R. Elton are worth studying, notably, *Reform and Reformation*, London, 1977; and *Policy and police*, Cambridge, 1972. The latter is particularly useful as a study of the means by which Thomas Cromwell enforced the Reformation. Penry Williams, *The Tudor regime*, Oxford, 1977, is an excellent alternative perspective. See also J. J. Scarisbrick, *Henry VIII*, London, 1968.

There are several good accounts of the mid-Tudor crisis and the reigns of Edward and Mary. Of these J. Loach and R. Tittler, *The mid-Tudor polity, 1540–1560*, London, 1980, fields a good selection of essays on aspects of the crisis. Nigel Heard, *Edward VI and Mary: a mid-Tudor Crisis?*, London, 1990, provides an effective short survey; and R. Tittler, *The reign of Mary I*, London, 1983, provides useful documentation on Mary I. See also Carolyn Erickson, *Bloody Mary: the life of Mary Tudor*, London, 1995.

An extremely effective and detailed discussion of both central and local politics is by S. J. Gunn, *Early Tudor government, 1485–1558*, London, 1995.

Penry Williams, *The later Tudors*, 1996, is an effective review of the era following Henry VIII, while Wallace Macaffrey, *Elizabeth I*, London, 1993, provides a rounded biography. Christopher Haigh, *Elizabeth I*, London, 1988; and Christopher Haigh (ed.), *The reign of Elizabeth I*, London, 1984, provide a good range of comments and discussion.

Reformation and religion

A. G. Dickens, *The English Reformation*, London, 1964, is still well worth reading, so, too, are J. J. Scarisbrick, *The English Reformation and the English people*, Oxford, 1984; E. Duffy, *The stripping of altars: traditional religion in England, 1450–1580*, New Haven, 1992; and Christopher Haigh (ed.) *The English Reformation*, Cambridge, 1987 edn, which give a fuller and revisionist view of proceedings. See also Robert Whiting, *The blind devotion of the people: Popular religion and the English Reformation*, Cambridge, 1989, which provides detailed discussion on the spread of the new religion; and Patrick Collinson, *The Elizabethan puritan movement*, London, 1967. A good collection of essays is to be found in Felicity Heal and Rosemary O'Day, *Church and society in England, Henry VIII to James I*, London, 1977. See also J. S. Block, *Factional politics and the English Reformation*, London, 1993; Gerald Bray (ed.), *Documents of the English Reformation*, London, 1994; David Loades, *Revolution in religion, the English Reformation*, London, 1992.

Order and disorder

Rebellion

A key text is A. Fletcher, *Tudor rebellions*, London, 1993, recently updated with D. MacCulloch co-editing. Also D. E. Underdown, *Revel, riot and rebellion: popular politics and culture in England, 1603–1660*, Oxford, 1985, is useful for the later period. See also David Loades, *Two Tudor conspiracies*, 1992. Lawrence Stone's *Crisis of the aristocracy*, Oxford, 1965, still provides useful details and insights into trouble among the nobility, as does Penry Williams, *Tudor regime*, Oxford 1977. For more detail on rebellions see S. Land, *Kett's rebellion*, London, 1977; M. L. Bush, *The Pilgrimage of Grace*, Manchester, 1996; Philip Caramani, *The Western Rebellion*, Tiverton, 1994; John Sturt, *Revolt in the west*, Exeter, 1987; John Fines, *The Pilgrimage of Grace*, London, 1986. For accounts of espionage and counter-espionage under Walsingham and Cecil, see Alison Plowden, *The Elizabethan secret service*, London, 1991; and Charles Nicholl, *The reckoning*, London, 1992.

General and parochial

There are several excellent collections of essays available on disorder in town and country. See Paul Griffiths, Adam Fox and Steve Hindle (eds.), *The experience of authority in early modern England*, London, 1996; A. Fletcher and J. Stevenson, *Order and disorder in early modern England*, Cambridge, 1985; and A. Fletcher and P. Roberts, *Religion, culture and society in early modern Britain*, Cambridge, 1994, which together collate a wide variety of the best research from the last two decades on a range of issues. See also J. A. Sharpe, *Early modern England: a social history, 1550–1750*, London, 1998; and K. Wrightson, *English society, 1580–1680*, London, 1982.

Witchcraft, religion and gender

Witchcraft is surprisingly central to many themes in the book as an issue as it takes in disorder, authority, religion and, conspicuously, gender.

Keith Thomas, *Religion and the decline of magic*, 1971, makes a wonderful starting point not only to study the witch-craze but a whole range of popular beliefs and superstitions. Alan Macfarlane, *Witchcraft in Tudor and Stuart England*, Oxford, 1973, provides a detailed analysis of the Essex witch-craze, while Hugh Trevor-Roper's old essay on *The European witch-craze of the sixteenth and seventeenth centuries*, London, 1969 is still useful. Recent revisionist work suggests that England had more in common with Europe than Thomas or Macfarlane thought and stress authority's distaste for witch crazes. See J. A. Sharpe, *Instruments of darkness: Witchcraft in England, 1550–1750*, London, 1996; Stuart Clark, *Thinking with demons, the idea of witchcraft in early modern Europe*, 1997; Marianne Hester (ed.), *Witchcraft in early modern Europe*, 1996, which provides a feminist insight. Finally, there is an excellent synthesis by Robin Briggs, *Witches and neighbours*, London, 1996.

On aspects of gender history, see Amanda Shephard, *Gender and authority in sixteenth century England*, 1994; Patricia Crawford, *Women and religion in England*, 1993; and Marianne Hester (ed.), *Women, violence and male power*, 1993. See also Lawrence Stone, *The family, sex and marriage in England, 1500–1800*, Oxford, 1977; A. Fletcher, *Gender, sex and subordination*, London, 1995; and Anne Laurence, *Women in England, 1500–1700*, London, 1994.

Poverty and vagrancy

John Pound, *Poverty and vagrancy in Tudor England*, London, 1971, provides useful sources and discussion, while A. L. Beier has provided two useful texts in the short paperback, *The problem of the poor in Tudor and Stuart England*, London, 1983; and the excellent, *Masterless men, the vagrancy problem in England, 1560–1640*, London, 1985. M. Spufford looks at the village communities in *The world of rural dissenters, 1520–1725*, 1995. See also Paul Slack, *Poverty and policy in Tudor and Stuart England*, London, 1988; and J. A. Sharpe, *Crime and society, 1550–1750*, London, 1984.

Glossary

attainders	Acts of Attainder were Acts passed by parliament declaring that certain individuals were guilty of treason and that their lands and possessions passed to the crown after their execution
beggary	the practice of begging (see also *indigence* and *vagrancy*)
benefit of clergy	the privilege, granted originally to all those in holy orders, of being tried in the church courts rather than in the ordinary law courts for criminal and civil offences
Brownists and Barrowists	extreme puritans, active in the 1580s and 1590s, who withdrew completely from their local parish churches and set up their own religious meeting houses
Calvinist	a word used to describe the teachings and practice of Calvin, the Swiss Protestant reformer based in Geneva
canon law	church law
charivari	a way of punishing scandalous members of the community – neighbours would make noisy demonstrations of disapproval
conciliar courts	courts, like the Star Chamber, that were staffed by members of the king's council
Court of High Commission	a *conciliar court* that dealt with matters connected with the doctrine and discipline of the Church of England
Dedham classis	a classis was an unofficial cell or meeting, within the established church, attended by those sympathetic to the Presbyterian services and form of church government – Dedham, a village in Suffolk, gave its name to a well-known classis
enclosure	the practice of enclosing open fields and common land with hedges and ditches, and turning them into individual holdings
engrossing	extending and consolidating estates often through *enclosure*
episcopal officers	bishops
Erastian	a word that describes a state in which the civil power or government controls the church
feudal incidents	unpredictable events, like the sudden death of a member of the nobility, which might, for example, allow the crown to administer the property of minors (wardship) and to arrange suitable marriages at a profit
general surveyors	officials, usually lawyers, appointed by the crown to monitor the activities, possessions and legal obligations of the nobility
Grand Juries	juries chosen from among the local magnates to try those accused of serious offences
impeachment	the process by which powerful officials were summoned and tried before parliament acting as a court of law

indigence	poverty (see also *beggary* and *vagrancy*)
justices of the peace	unpaid magistrates chosen from among the local gentry to enforce the law
justiceship	the post of justice of the peace
maintenance	the interference by the lord in the local law courts to maintain or support a follower or his cause
missionary priests	those Catholic priests trained at the seminary at Douai who arrived in England in the 1570s to convert the English back to Roman Catholicism; by the 1580s, Jesuit missionary priests were also working in England
non-residence	the absence of holders of multiple church offices from their sees or monasteries
occasional conformity	the practice by which people would go to church just often enough to avoid the *recusancy* fines
papal bull	an official decree issued by the pope
Plantagenet	the dynasty of kings that ruled England in the fourteenth century
predestination	the belief that God had predestined some people to salvation while permitting others to suffer eternal damnation
prelates	bishops
presbyter	a minister or elder who headed each Presbyterian congregation
prophesyings	meetings of local clergy in Elizabeth's reign to hear one another preach
recusancy laws	laws that laid down a series of fines for recusants, that is those, particularly Catholics, who deliberately absented themselves from the services of the Established church
retaining	the feudal right and obligation of the nobility to keep armed men (retainers) for military service – they were usually dressed in a distinctive livery
rough music	see *charivari*
royal demesne	land owned by the monarch
sheriff	a local law officer who received a salary
simony	the practice of accepting payment for religious services such as saying Mass
sumptuary laws	laws restricting the kind of clothes or the types of weapons that people could possess, according to their social rank
the Pale	the area around Dublin that was under the direct control of English officials appointed by the crown
theocracies	those states in which the church holds political as well as spiritual power
three propositions	Whitgift tested his clergy according to their willingness to express belief in three propositions taken from the Thirty-nine Articles – if the clergy rejected these, they could be excluded from their parishes
vagrancy	the practice adopted by the poor of wandering around the country in search of work or better-paid employment (see also *beggary* and *indigence*)
Zwinglian	a word used to describe the teachings and practice of Zwingli, a Swiss Protestant reformer of the sixteenth century

Chronology

1485 *22 August:* Henry Tudor defeats Richard III at the Battle of Bosworth.
7 November: Henry VII is crowned.

1486 Henry marries Elizabeth of York.

1487 *24 May:* Lambert Simnel is crowned as Edward VI in Ireland.
16 June: The Battle of Stoke finally ends the Wars of the Roses.

1489 A revolt breaks out over taxation and the duke of Northumberland is killed.

1491 An army is sent to Ireland.

1493 A seven-year truce is made with Scotland.

1494 Poynings' Law prohibits any bill being introduced by the Irish parliament without prior royal approval.

1495 Perkin Warbeck lands in England.
The Act against Vagabonds and Beggars is passed.

1496 Perkin Warbeck and the Scots invade England.
A commercial treaty, the *Intercursus Magnus*, is signed with Burgundy.

1497 A rebellion breaks out in Cornwall over taxation.
Perkin Warbeck is captured.

1499 Perkin Warbeck and the earl of Warwick are executed.

1501 Prince Arthur and Catherine of Aragon are married.

1502 Arthur dies.

1503 James IV of Scotland and Margaret Tudor are married.

1504 The Act against Illegal Retainers is passed.

1509 Henry VII dies, Henry VIII succeeds and, in June, marries Catherine of Aragon.

1513 The English defeat the French at the Battle of the Spurs and occupy Tournai.
The English defeat the Scots at the Battle of Flodden, in which James IV and his heir are killed.

1514 Church courts imprison Richard Hunne for heresy.

1516 Mary Tudor is born.

1517 Thomas Wolsey sets up the Enclosure Commission.

1518 The Treaty of London (the Universal Peace) is signed.

1520 Henry VIII and Francis I of France meet at the 'Field of the Cloth of Gold'.

1521 The duke of Buckingham is executed for treason.

1525 The Amicable Grant is levied to pay for war with France, provoking open resistance.

1527 Henry VIII decides to divorce Catherine of Aragon.

1529	The Legatine Court meets to consider the royal divorce.
1529–36	Henry's Reformation Parliament meets seven times during this period.
1530	Wolsey dies.
1531	The Act for the Punishment of Beggars is passed.
1532	The Act for the Submission of Clergy recognises Henry's superiority over ecclesiastical matters. Henry appoints Thomas Cranmer archbishop of Canterbury.
1533	Thomas Cromwell becomes chief minister. *January:* Henry marries Anne Boleyn in secret. Elizabeth I is born. The Act in Restraint of Appeals is passed by parliament.
1534	The Act of Supremacy and the Treasons Act are passed. Elizabeth Barton, the Nun of Kent, is executed for treason. The Irish revolt, led by Thomas Fitzgerald, Lord Offaly.
1535	Royal commissions survey all church property in England and Wales and the *Valor Ecclesiasticus* is compiled. *July:* Thomas More and John Fisher refuse to accept Henry's claim to be Supreme Head of the Church and are executed.
1536	The Act for the Dissolution of the Lesser Monasteries is passed. Catherine of Aragon dies. Anne Boleyn is executed. The Act of Union incorporating Wales into England is passed. The Act punishing Sturdy Beggars is passed. The Ten Articles are published. Henry marries Jane Seymour. *October:* The Pilgrimage of Grace begins.
1537	Edward VI is born. Jane Seymour dies.
1538	Cromwell orders a copy of the English translation of the Bible to be placed in every parish church. France and the Holy Roman Empire are at peace so there is an invasion scare in England. Dissolutions of the larger monasteries begin. The judicial murders of the Pole family begin.
1539	The Act of Six Articles provokes a religious reaction.
1540	Henry marries Anne of Cleves in January and divorces her in July. He then marries Catherine Howard. Thomas Cromwell is executed. War breaks out with France.
1541	Henry is declared King of Ireland.
1542	Catherine Howard is executed for adultery. James V of Scotland dies at Battle of Solway Moss.
1543	Henry marries Catherine Parr. The Treaty of Greenwich is made with the Scots. War breaks out again with France. *The King's book* is published.

1544   The English invade France and occupy Boulogne.
The 'rough wooing' begins in Scotland.

1546   Anne Askew is tried and executed.
Catherine Parr is accused of heresy.
The Howard family falls from favour.

1547   Henry, earl of Surrey, is executed.
The duke of Norfolk is condemned.
Henry dies and Edward VI succeeds.
Edward's uncle, the duke of Somerset, becomes Lord Protector.
The Heresy Laws and the Chantries Act are repealed.
The Vagabonds (Slave) Act is passed.

1548   John Hales introduces the Enclosure Bills and sets up a commission to enquire into the effects of enclosure.

1549   The First Edwardian Prayer Book is published.
Parliament passes the Act of Uniformity.
The Cornish Rebellion takes place.
Kett's Rebellion takes place in East Anglia.
The privy council overthrows the duke of Somerset.

1552   The Poor Law Act of 1547 is moderated.
The Second Edwardian Prayer Book is published.

1553   Edward VI dies. Northumberland places Lady Jane Grey on the throne.
After nine days, Mary Tudor succeeds.

1554   A marriage treaty is made with Philip II of Spain.
The Anti-heresy Laws are restored.

1555   Wyatt is executed after his rebellion fails.
The burning of heretics begins.

1558   Calais falls to France.
Mary Tudor dies and Elizabeth I succeeds.

1559   The Acts of Supremacy and Uniformity are passed. The Church of England is restored but the Catholic interpretation of the Mass is compromised.
The Treaty of Cateau-Cambrésis is signed.

1559–60   The Scottish Reformation begins. English forces assist against the French party in Scotland.

1561   Mary Queen of Scots returns to Scotland.

1562–63   Elizabeth is ill with smallpox, causing concern for the succession.

1563   Parliament articulates fears over marriage and the succession.
The Act for Poor Relief, the Statute of Artificers and the Witchcraft Act are passed.
The Tillage Act is passed.

1565–66   The controversy over the wearing of Church vestments rages.

1565   Mary Queen of Scots marries Lord Darnley.

1567   Mary is involved in the murder of Darnley and is forced to abdicate.

1568   Mary Queen of Scots flees to England and becomes a focus for plots against Elizabeth.

The duke of Alva's treasure is impounded.
A Catholic seminary is founded at Douai.

1569 The Revolt of the Northern Earls takes place.

1570 The papal bull, *Regnans in Excelsis*, excommunicates Elizabeth and urges Catholic resistance.

1571 The Ridolfi Plot is revealed.
The Treasons Act is passed.

1572 Thomas Howard, duke of Norfolk, is executed.
The St Bartholomew's Eve Massacre of Huguenots in France takes place.
The Act for Punishment of Vagabonds is passed.

1573 Thomas Walsingham is appointed Secretary of State.

1575 Edmund Grindal is appointed archbishop of Canterbury.

1576 Grindal is suspended for refusing to suppress prophesyings.
The Act for Setting the Poor to Work is passed.

1577 The Fitzmaurice Rebellion begins in Ireland.

1579 The Desmond Rebellion takes place in Munster.

1580 Campion and Parsons arrive in England.

1583 The Throckmorton Plot is revealed.
John Whitgift becomes archbishop of Canterbury.

1584 William of Orange is murdered.
The earl of Leicester is sent to the Netherlands.
The Bond of Association calls on all Englishmen to protect the life of the queen.

1586 Mary Queen of Scots is implicated in the Babington Plot.
The English fleet attacks Cadiz.

1587 Mary Queen of Scots is executed at Fotheringhay.

1588 Philip II adopts Mary Queen of Scots' claim to the throne.
The Spanish Armada is defeated.
Robert Dudley, earl of Leicester, dies.

1588–89 The Matthew Marprelate Tracts are published.

1590 Sir Francis Walsingham dies.

1593 The Act against Sectaries and Brownists.

1594 The earl of Tyrone leads Irish rebellion against English rule.

1597 A further Tillage Act is passed.
The Acts for Relief of the Poor and for the Punishment of Rogues are passed.

1598 William Cecil, Lord Burghley, dies.

1601 The earl of Essex is executed.
New Poor Law legislation creates overseers of the poor to raise money and create jobs.
Spanish troops land at Kinsale in Ireland.

1603 Elizabeth dies and James I succeeds.
Tyrone surrenders, ending the Irish War.

Index

absolutism, 6, 8–9
adolescents, *see* young people
agrarian problems, 46, 52, 54–7, 92, 105
Amicable Grant, 91, 93
armies, 4–6, 87–8; private, 2, 3–4, 14
Aske, Robert, 4, 5, 27, 42, 91, 93, 95, 98
Askew, Anne, 27, 38, 80
Audley, Thomas, 19
Aylmer, John, bishop of London, 35

Barton, Elizabeth, 27, 38, 80
Beattie, John, 31
beggars, 35–6, 41, 54
Beier, A. L., 40, 41
Bess of Hardwicke, 32
binding over (to keep the peace), 84
Black Death, 38, 41
Body, William, 94, 95, 100
Boleyn, Anne, 17, 33, 34, 47, 48, 67, 73, 91
Bond of Association, 87
Bosworth, Battle of (1485), 1, 13
Buckingham, Edward Stafford, duke of, 58

Campion, Edmund, 73, 102
canon law, 23
Capp, Bernard, 32
Caramani, Philip, 94
Carew, Sir Peter, 13, 55, 62, 95, 96
Cartwright, Thomas, 80
Cathars, 27, 34
Catherine of Aragon, 34, 47, 91, 93, 100
Catholicism, 22, 24, 27; and Elizabeth I, 28, 69, 72–4, 78; and the mid-Tudor crisis, 48, 49–50, 50–1, 53, 54; survival of in the North, 101–2; and the witch-craze, 40
Cecil, William (later Lord Burghley), 68, 74, 78, 86, 100, 109
children, attitudes to, 36
church, the, 8, 9, 22–30; and the attitude of the government to dissent, 27–8; and the clergy, 15, 23, 33, 78, 79–80; Elizabethan, 24, 67, 69, 78–80, 104, 107; exhortation concerning good order and obedience, 42–3, 49; impact on society of, 22; law and government, 23; and the mid-Tudor crisis, 46, 47, 48–52, 53–4; and morality, 33–4; parish churches and priests, 14, 15; *see also* Catholicism; Protestantism; Reformation

class: and legalism, 84, 85; and marriage, 33; and rebellions, 95, 100; and the Reformation, 26; and social control, 39, 40
classis movement, 79
Coke, Sir Edward, 73
commissions, Elizabethan, 107–8
community welfare, and the parish, 15–16
Cornish Rebellion (1549), 26, 50, 52, 55, 90–1, 94
Council in the Marches of Wales, 58, 59, 109
courts, 11–13, 18, 83
Cranmer, Thomas, 23, 24, 25, 27, 46, 48, 49, 50, 51
Crawford, Patricia, 38
crime: increase in levels of, 104–5; punishment of, 15, 38–9, 76, 105, 109
Cromwell, Thomas, 12–13, 15, 47, 48, 54, 108; and the church, 23, 24, 25, 50, 107; and the development of early modern government, 17–18, 19, 45, 68; fall of, 29; and the government of Wales, 58, 59; and Ireland, 60; and the Pilgrimage of Grace (1536–37), 93, 94, 101; and sources of opposition, 8

Danvers, Sir Richard, 12
Desmond rising (Ireland), 62
Dickens, A. G., 23, 81
discipline, 35–7, 76
Divine Right, 3
divorce, 33
Drake, Sir Francis, 67, 71
duelling, 85
Duffy, E., 23, 24

economic problems, 15–16, 52–3
education, 18, 36–7, 76, 85, 108
Edward IV, King, 2, 3, 6, 10, 11, 14, 16, 22, 33, 47
Edward VI, King, 24, 28, 45, 88; and the church, 46, 50–1
Elizabeth I, Queen, 67–77; accession to the throne, 45, 46, 67; administration under, 68–9; and Catholics, 28, 69, 72–4, 78; and the church, 24, 67, 69, 78–80, 104, 107; and crown finances, 109; excommunication of (1570), 72–3; foreign policy of, 67, 70–1; government of, 108–9; and male attitudes to women, 32, 35; and Mary Queen of Scots, 8,